Illustrated
MATH
DICTIONARY

An Essential Student Resource

Judith de Klerk

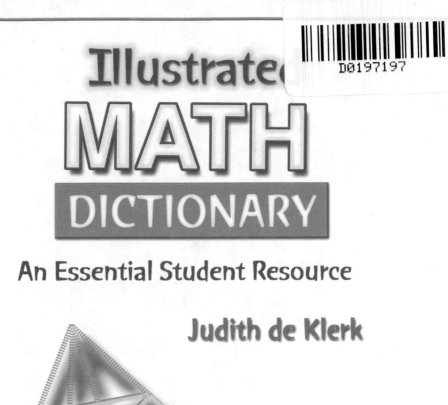

GLOBE FEARON
Pearson Learning Group

Cover Design: Elaine Lopez

Interior Illustrations: Pat Kermode

Design Manager: M. Jane Heelan

Executive Editor: Judith Adams

Adapted from *Illustrated Maths Dictionary*, 3rd edition, published 1999 by
Pearson Education Australia Pty Limited.

ISBN 0-673-59959-0
Printed in the United States of America

    13 14 15   10 09 08 07

Globe
Fearon
Pearson Learning Group

1-800-321-3106
www.pearsonlearning.com

Contents

Introduction

The language of mathematics often confuses children, and it is sometimes difficult for the teacher to explain the meaning of mathematical terms simply but accurately.

This new revised edition offers an up-to-date dictionary of math terms used in elementary and middle schools. The definitions are written in simple language that children can understand, yet are clear, precise, and concise. The terms are supported by hundreds of examples and illustrations.

This is essentially a dictionary for students, but I hope that teachers and parents will also find it helpful.

Judith de Klerk

a

(i) The letter A stands for area in formulas.

Example: Area of a triangle

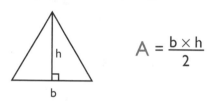

$$A = \frac{b \times h}{2}$$

(ii) A, and other letters, are used to name points, lines, angles and corners (vertices) of polygons and solids.

Examples:

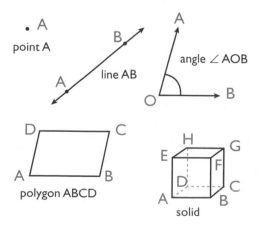

point A

line AB

angle ∠ AOB

polygon ABCD

solid

See *angle name, area, formula, line, point, vertex.*

abacus

Usually a board with pegs or a frame with wires on which discs, beads, or counters are placed. Used for counting and calculating.

Examples:

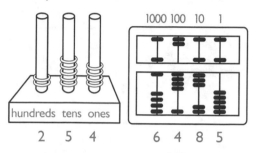

abbreviation

A shortened form of writing words and phrases.

When writing shortened forms of words, we often put periods after the letters.

Example:
United States: U.S.

accurate

Exact, correct, right, without error.

Note: Measurements are not exact. We usually measure to the nearest unit, therefore our answers are only approximate. For example, if we say something is 30 cm long, we mean nearer to 30 cm than to either 31 cm or 29 cm.

See *approximately.*

acute

Sharp. Sharply pointed.
(i) acute angle
     A sharply pointed angle with size
     less than a right angle (<90°).

Example:

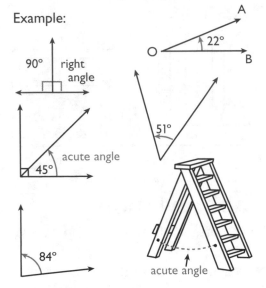

See *angle, right angle.*

(ii) acute triangle
A triangle with all three inside
angles being acute.

Example:

acute triangle

See *equilateral triangle, obtuse triangle, right
triangle, scalene triangle.*

add

Join two or more numbers or
quantities together.

Example:

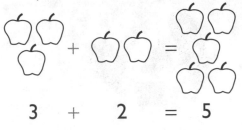

$$3 \quad + \quad 2 \quad = \quad 5$$

The apples were added together.
See *addition, quantity.*

addend

Any number that is to be added.

$$2 \quad + \quad 6 \quad = \quad 8$$

addend   addend   sum

In $2 + 6 = 8$, 2 and 6 are addends;
8 is the sum.

addition

The symbol for addition is +.
(i) Joining the values of two or
     more numbers together.

$$3 + 7 = 10$$

(ii) On the number line.

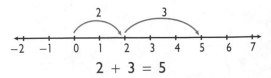

$$2 + 3 = 5$$

(iii) Addition of fractions.

$$\frac{1}{4} + \frac{3}{5} = \frac{5+12}{20} = \frac{17}{20}$$

(iv) Addition of integers.

$$^+5 + {}^-7 = {}^-2$$

(v) Addition of algebraic terms.

$$2a + 3b + 5a = 7a + 3b$$

See fraction, integer, number line.

addition property of zero

When zero is added to any number, the sum is the same as the number.

Examples:

$$4 + 0 = 4$$
$$0 + 12 = 12$$

See sum, zero.

additive inverse

When we add a number and its inverse, the answer is zero.

Example:

$$8 + {}^-8 = 0$$
$$\text{number} \quad \text{inverse}$$

See inverse, zero.

adjacent

Positioned next to each other, having a common point or side.

Example:

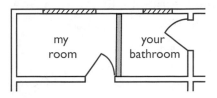

My room is adjacent to your bathroom.

(i) Adjacent sides.

In this triangle side AB is adjacent to side AC because they have a common vertex A.

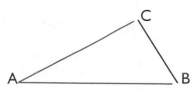

(ii) Adjacent angles.

Two angles positioned in the same plane that have a common side and a common vertex.

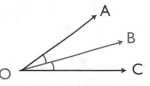

$\angle$AOB is adjacent to $\angle$BOC because they have a common side $\overrightarrow{OB}$.

See plane, vertex.

algebra

Part of mathematics that studies number systems and number properties. In algebra we use numerals, symbols, or letters, called variables, to stand for the unknown values.

Examples:

$$\maltese + \maltese = 2\,\maltese$$
$$5 - x$$
$$a + b + c$$
$$x^2 - 2xy + y$$

See *coefficient, numeral, symbol, variable.*

algorithm

A rule for solving a problem in a certain number of steps.
Every step is clearly described.

Example:
Use blocks to find the product of 3×4.

Step 1 Lay down one group of four ones.

Step 2 Put down the second and third groups of four.

Step 3 Regroup 10 ones as one ten.

Step 4 Write the product. $3 \times 4 = 12$

See *base ten blocks.*

align

Lay, place in a straight line.

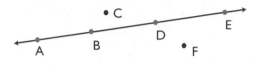

Points A, B, D, and E are aligned, points C and F are not.

See *line.*

alternate angles

See *parallel lines.*

altitude

Height. How high something is above the surface of the earth, sea level or horizon. Altitude is the length of perpendicular height from base to vertex.

Example:

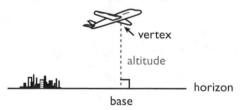

The altitude of this airplane is 9,000 meters.

See *height, perpendicular height, surface.*

a.m.

(ante meridiem)

The time from immediately after midnight until immediately before noon.

Example:

It is morning.
The time is five past five.
It is 5:05 a.m.

See *p.m.*

amount

An amount of something means
how much of that thing.

Example:
The amount of money in my pocket

analog clock

A clock or a watch that has
numerals 1–12 on its face, and two
hands pointing at them to show
the time.

Example:

This clock shows twenty-five minutes
past nine in the morning.
It is 9:25 a.m.

See *a.m., digital clock, p.m.*

angle

The space between two straight
lines with a common endpoint
(vertex).

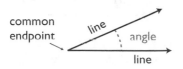

An angle is the amount of turn of
a ray about a fixed point.

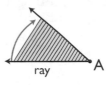

Angle is the inclination of two lines
to each other.

Angles are measured in degrees (°),
minutes (') and seconds (").

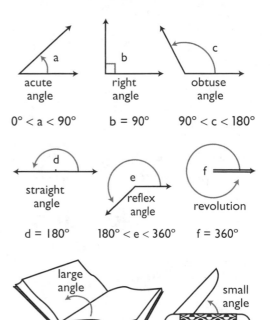

acute angle   right angle   obtuse angle

$0° < a < 90°$ $b = 90°$ $90° < c < 180°$

straight angle   reflex angle   revolution

$d = 180°$ $180° < e < 360°$ $f = 360°$

large angle   small angle

See *acute angle, degree, obtuse angle,
parallel lines, ray, reflex angle, revolution, right
angle, straight angle.*

angle name

Angles are given names by marking them with letters.

Example:

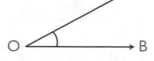

The name of this angle is <AOB. The letter O in the middle (<AOB) indicates the common endpoint.

angle of depression
(of an object)

An angle formed between the horizontal line and the line of sight to an object below.

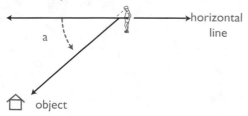

Angle a is the angle of depression.
See *angle of elevation.*

angle of elevation

An angle formed between the horizontal line and the line of sight to an object above.

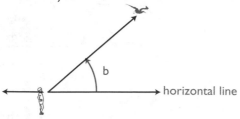

Angle b is the angle of elevation.
See *angle of depression.*

angle sum

The total amount of degrees in any polygon.

(i) Angle sum of a triangle is 180°.

$\angle$ a + $\angle$ b + $\angle$ c = 180°

(ii) Angle sum of a quadrilateral is 360°.

4 × 90° = 360°

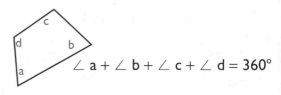

$\angle$ a + $\angle$ b + $\angle$ c + $\angle$ d = 360°

(iii) Angle sum of any polygon may be found:

number of vertices × 180° − 360°,
or
(number of vertices − 2) × 180°

Examples:

triangle	(3 × 180°) − 360° = 180°
or	(3 − 2) × 180° = 180°
pentagon	(5 − 2) × 180° = 540°
hexagon	(6 × 180°) − 360° = 720°

annual

(i) Happening only once a year.
Example: Annual flower show.

(ii) Recurring yearly.
Example: annual rate of interest is 6.5%.

See *per annum, percent.*

annulus

The area between two concentric circles.

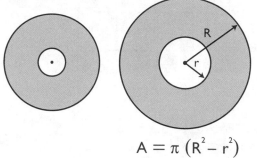

$$A = \pi \left(R^2 - r^2 \right)$$

See *area, circle, concentric circles*.

apex

The highest point where two or more lines meet to form a corner of a figure or solid. The apex is the furthest vertical distance from the base.

Examples:

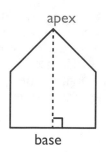

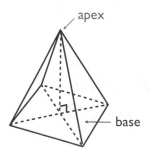

See *vertex, pyramid*.

approximately

(Symbol: ≈)

Nearly, not exactly, but almost. The symbol ≈ may be used for "is approximately equal to."

Example:

The expression
0.97 ≈ 1
means "0.97 is approximately equal to 1."

See *rounding, accurate*.

approximation

(Symbol: ≈)

A result that is nearly, not exactly, but almost accurate. One method of approximation is calculating with rounded figures.

Examples:
(i) 798 × 2.1 ≈ 800 × 2 ≈ 1,600
(ii) The value of 3.14 for π is only an approximation.

See *accurate, approximately, rounding*.

Arabic numerals

1, 2, 3, 4, 5, … Now in common use in all western countries.

See *Hindu–Arabic*.

arc

A part of any curve, but most often used to mean a part of a circle.

Example:

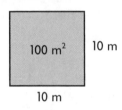

See *circle, curve.*

are

Unit of area in the metric system. It is the area of a square with sides measuring ten meters.

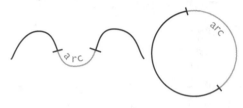

100 m² = 1 are
100 are = 1 ha

See *area, hectare.*

area

The amount of surface or the size of a surface.

Area is measured in square units. Some units of area are:

square foot	ft²
square meter	m²
square mile	mi²
square kilometer	km²

Example:

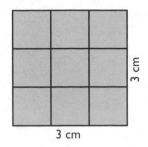

The area of this shape is
length x width
3 cm x 3 cm = 9 cm²

See *conservation of area, surface, unit of measurement, formula.*

arithmetic

The part of mathematics concerned with the study of numbers.

Arithmetic is used for computation with whole numbers, fractions, and decimals. The computations include addition, subtraction, multiplication, and division. Arithmetic is also used for measuring, solving word problems, and working with money.

See *computation.*

arithmetic mean

See *average, mean.*

arithmetic progression

See *progression.*

array

Arrangement of objects, numbers, etc., in columns or rows.

Examples:

An array of objects in rows and columns

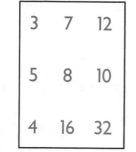

These numbers form an array.

arrow

Used to indicate direction.

Example: weather vane

arrow diagram

A diagram using arrows to show a relation (or connection) between one thing and another.

Examples:

(i) Relation in one set of numbers.

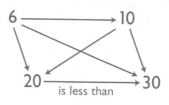

is less than

(ii) Relation between two sets.

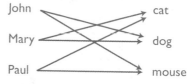

PETS CHILDREN HAVE

John   cat
Mary   dog
Paul   mouse

See *mapping, many-to-one correspondence, one-to-one correspondence, relation, set.*

ascending order

Going upwards or increasing in value.

Examples:
These numbers are in ascending order:

0.1, 0.2, 0.3, 0.4, 0.5

least   greatest

These lengths have been arranged in ascending order:

5 cm, 50 cm, 5 m, 5 km, 50 km

shortest   longest

See *descending order, increase, order, pattern, sequence.*

associative property of addition

When three or more numbers are added, changing the way the numbers are grouped does not change the answer (sum).

Example:
$$3 + 7 + 9$$
$$= (3 + 7) + 9$$
$$= \quad 10 \quad + 9 = 19$$

or

$$3 + (7 + 9)$$
$$= 3 + \quad 16 \quad = 19$$

See *commutative property of addition, sum.*

associative property of multiplication

When three or more numbers are multiplied, changing the way the numbers are grouped does not change the answer (product).

Example:
$$3 \times 7 \times 9$$
$$= (3 \times 7) \times 9$$
$$= \quad 21 \quad \times 9$$
$$= 189$$

or

$$3 \times (7 \times 9)$$
$$= 3 \times \quad 63$$
$$= 189$$

See *commutative property of multiplication, product.*

asterisk

A small star * used to mark a space where something is missing.

Examples:

$3 * 2 = 6$ * means $\times$ (multiply)

$3 * 2 = 5$ * means $+$ (add)

$3 * 2 = 1$ * means $-$ (subtract)

$3 * 2 = 1.5$ * means $\div$ (divide)

asymmetry

Not having symmetry. An object that has no line symmetry is described as asymmetrical.

Examples:
The butterfly is symmetrical.

This picture of a toy tractor is asymmetrical.

See *line of symmetry, symmetry.*

attribute

A characteristic of an object.

Examples: shape, size, color.

(i) Attributes of shape:
round, square, hexagonal ... Round and thin

(ii) Attributes of size:
thick, thin, small, big ...
Round and thick and white

(iii) Attributes of color:
black, red, yellow ...

See *classify, property.*

Square and black

average

The average of a collection of numbers is found by adding all the numbers and dividing the sum by the number of addends.

Example:

Find the average of 2, 5, 4, 6 and 3.

$$\text{Average} = \frac{\text{sum}}{\text{number of addends}}$$

$$= \frac{2 + 5 + 4 + 6 + 3}{5}$$

$$= \frac{20}{5}$$

Average   =   4

This is also called the mean or arithmetic mean.

See *mean, score, sum.*

axis

(Plural: axes)

(i)   The lines that form the framework for a graph. The horizontal axis is called x-axis; the vertical axis is called y-axis. Both axes are marked with equally spaced scales. The point where the axes intersect is called the origin (O).

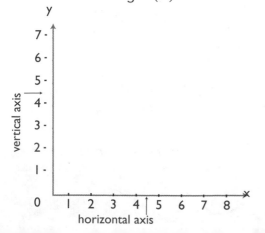

Axes are sometimes called:
x-axis = abscissa
y-axis = ordinate

(ii)   A line that divides a figure or solid into two matching halves. Also called an axis of symmetry or a line of symmetry.

Examples:

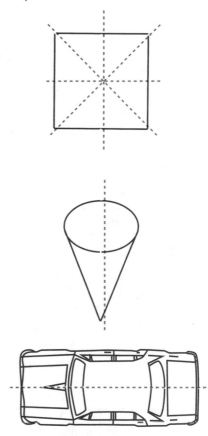

See *coordinates, graph, horizontal, intersection, line of symmetry, origin, vertical.*

axis of symmetry

See *line of symmetry.*

bar graph

A graph that uses horizontal or vertical bars to represent various kinds of information.

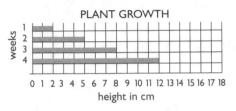

PLANT GROWTH

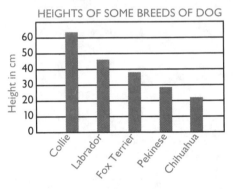

HEIGHTS OF SOME BREEDS OF DOG

See *graph, pie chart, pictograph.*

balance

(i) An equal distribution.

balanced   unbalanced

(ii) Balance scale is a name given to some kinds of scales used for weighing things.

Example:

a spring
balance

(iii) The amount of money in a bank account.

Date	Description	Credit	Debit	Balance
2001				
Feb 02	Pay	350		
Feb 05	ATM withdrawal		200	150
Feb 10	Rent		50	100
Feb 16	Pay	350		450
Feb 21	Taxes		295	155

base

(i) The face on which a shape or a solid stands.

Examples:

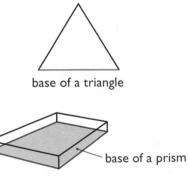

base of a triangle

base of a prism

(ii) The number on which a place value system of numeration is constructed.

Example:

The Hindu–Arabic system is a base 10 system.

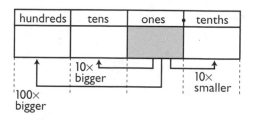

hundreds	tens	ones	tenths

10× bigger

100× bigger

10× smaller

(iii) A number, symbol, or variable shown with an exponent.

Examples:

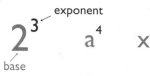

exponent

$$2^3 \qquad a^4 \qquad x^a$$

base

In exponential notation, the base is the number read first.
2^3 is read *two cubed,* or *two to the third power.* 2 is called the base.
See *decimal place-value system, exponent, power of a number.*

base line

(i) The horizontal axis of a graph.

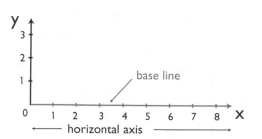

base line

horizontal axis

(ii) A base from which the heights of objects may be compared.

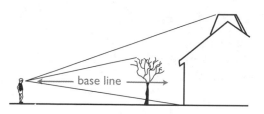

base line

See *axis, horizontal line.*

base ten blocks

A set of blocks used to give a concrete representation of numbers.

Example:
A set of base ten blocks consists of:

small cubes – units or ones

tens – 10 small cubes joined together

hundreds – 100 small cubes formed into a square

thousands – 1,000 small cubes, formed into a large cube

See *base.*

base ten system

See *decimal place-value system, decimal system, index, index notation, power of a number.*

basic facts

Operations performed with one-digit numbers 0, 1, 2, 3, 4, 5, 6, 7, 8, and 9.

Examples:

Addition
$0 + 0 = 0$ $0 + 1 = 1$
$1 + 1 = 2$ $9 + 9 = 18$

Subtraction corresponds with addition.

Multiplication
$0 \times 0 = 0$ $0 \times 1 = 0$
$1 \times 1 = 1$ $9 \times 9 = 81$

Division corresponds with multiplication.

(Note: It is not possible to divide by zero!)

See *digit, operation, zero*.

beam balance

Any balance where a beam is used.

Examples:

a seesaw   a beam balance

A beam balance is used to measure the mass of an object by balancing it with an object whose mass is known.

See *balance, mass*.

bearing

A horizontal angle measured from 0° to 90° between a north or south direction and the direction of the object.

True bearings are measured to the true north direction, magnetic bearings to the magnetic north (or south).

Example:

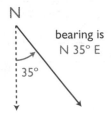

N

bearing is N 35° E

35°

See *compass, direction*.

bicentennial

200th anniversary.

Example:
1976 marked the bicentennial of the signing of the Declaration of Independence.

billion

A billion is one thousand millions.

$1{,}000{,}000{,}000$ or (10^9)

binary

A base-2 number system that uses only 0 and 1 to represent numbers. It is the smallest number system used to represent information. All numbers can be represented in a binary system.

Example:
Binary (Base-2) system.

Place value	a^7	a^6	a^5	a^4	a^3	a^2	a^1	a^0	Number
Binary	2^7	2^6	2^5	2^4	2^3	2^2	2^1	2^0	
Value	128	64	32	16	8	4	2	1	
								0	0
							0	1	1
							1	0	2
						0	1	1	3
					0	1	0	0	4
				0	1	0	1	0	10
				0	1	1	1	1	15
			0	1	1	0	0	1	25
	1	0	0	0	1	1	0	0	140

binomial

In algebra, an expression consisting of two terms joined by $+$ or $-$. The terms are called monomials.

Examples:

$$2 + a \qquad 3a - b \qquad 2x^2 + y^2$$

See *algebra*.

bisect

To cut or divide into two equal parts.
This angle has been bisected.

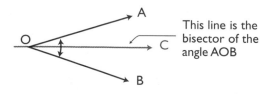

This line is the bisector of the angle AOB

$$\angle\,AOC = \angle COB$$

bisector

A straight line that divides an angle, or an interval, into two equal parts.

Examples:

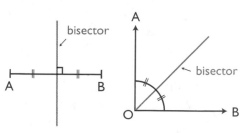

See *bisect, interval, midpoint*.

boundary

A line around the edge of a region.

Examples:

(i)   The boundary around a soccer field.

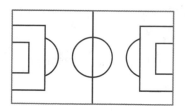

(ii)   A boundary of a hexagon is its perimeter.

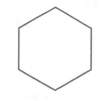

See *perimeter, region*.

brackets

The signs $(\,)\,[\;]\,\{\,\}$ are used for grouping things or numbers together.

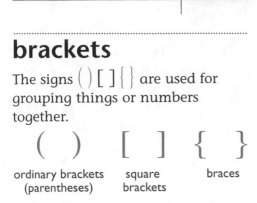

ordinary brackets   square   braces
(parentheses)   brackets

Brackets are used to indicate the order of operations.

Example:

$5\{2\,[4(3+10)-(35\div5)-8]\}$

$=5\{2\,[(4\times13)-7-8]\}$ ① remove ordinary brackets

$=5\{2\,[52-15]\}$ ② remove square brackets

$=5\{2\times37\}$ ③ remove braces

$=5\times74=370$

See grouping symbols, order of operations.

budget

A plan for using money.

Example:

Jessica earns $196 a week. Her budget is:

Rent and food	$85
Bus fares	$16
Clothes	$25
Entertainment	$30
Savings	$40
Total	$196

C

(i) C is a symbol for Celsius temperature scale.

0°C   water freezes

100°C water boils

(ii) A symbol for circumference in formulas.

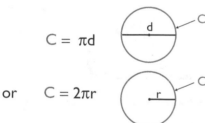

C = πd

or   C = 2πr

(iii) In Roman numerals, C stands for one hundred.

CCCXXII = 322

calculate

Work out the answer. Use mathematical procedures to determine a number, quantity, or expression.

calculator

Calculating aid. Calculators are electronic. They are battery- or solar-powered.

calendar

A calendar represents the way in which a year is broken up into months, weeks and days.

Example:

2000

January						
M	T	W	T	F	S	S
31					1	2
3	4	5	6	7	8	9
10	11	12	13	14	15	16
17	18	19	20	21	22	23
24	25	26	27	28	29	30

The third Tuesday in February 2000 was the 15th.

See *day, leap year, month, year.*

February						
M	T	W	T	F	S	S
	1	2	3	4	5	6
7	8	9	10	11	12	13
14	(15)	16	17	18	19	20
21	22	23	24	25	26	27
28	29					

calliper

A measuring instrument with curved legs for measuring thickness (diameter) of curved (convex) objects or, turned outwards, for measuring cavities.

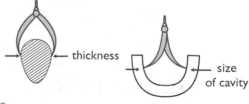

thickness

size of cavity

See *concave, convex.*

canceling

A method of changing a fraction to lower terms.

Examples:

(i) Divide both numerator and denominator by three (common factor).

$$\frac{15 \div 3}{21 \div 3} = \frac{\cancel{15}\ ^5}{\cancel{21}\ ^7} = \frac{5}{7}$$

(ii) Use canceling to multiply.

$$\frac{^3\cancel{15}}{_2\cancel{22}} \times \frac{\cancel{33}\ ^3}{\cancel{40}\ _8} = \frac{3 \times 3}{2 \times 8} = \frac{9}{16}$$

See *denominator, fraction, numerator, simple fraction, simplify.*

capacity

How much a container can hold. The number of cubic units a container can hold is called its capacity or volume.

Example:

An eye dropper holds about 1 milliliter of liquid, which fills one cubic centimeter.

See *volume.*

cardinal number

The number of all elements (members) in a set. When we count, we give each element one number, starting with 1. These numbers are in sequence. The last number given is the cardinal number of the set.

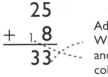

Example:

How many balloons?

The cardinal number of this set of balloons is 5.

See *counting, sequence, set.*

carrying

Another word for regrouping.

Example:

$$\begin{array}{r} 25 \\ + \ 1\ 8 \\ \hline 33 \end{array}$$

Add $5 + 8 = 13$.
Write 3 in ones column, and carry 1 into tens column

See *regroup.*

Cartesian coordinates

See *coordinates.*

Celsius scale

See *C, degree Celsius, temperature.*

cent

(Symbol:¢)

One cent is one hundredth of a dollar.

$$1¢ = \$0.01$$

$$\$1 = 100¢$$

See *dollar.*

Centigrade

Former name of metric temperature scale. We now call it the Celsius scale.

See *degree Celsius, temperature.*

centimeter

(Symbol: cm)

A unit of length.

1 cm = 0.01 m

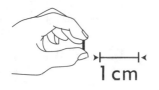

1 cm

100 cm = 1 m

Example:

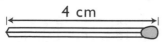

4 cm

This match is four centimeters long.

See *length, unit of measurement.*

center

A point that is the same distance from all points of a circle, a sphere, etc.

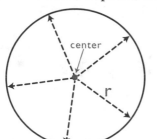

center

r

The distance is called radius (r).

See *circle, circumference, radius.*

century

There are one hundred years in a century.

chance

A likelihood of an event happening.

See *probability.*

chance event

An event for which the outcome is uncertain.

For some events we can predict a possible outcome, but we can never be sure.

Examples:

Tossing a coin, rolling a die, drawing a colored marble from a bag.

See *probability.*

checking

A way of making sure that an answer is correct. One way of checking is by using the inverse operation.

Examples:
(i) Subtraction is checked
     by addition.

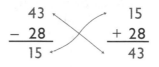

$$43 \qquad\qquad 15$$
$$- \ 28 \qquad\qquad + \ 28$$
$$\overline{\quad 15 \quad} \qquad\qquad \overline{\quad 43 \quad}$$

The answer 15 is correct.

(ii) Division is checked by multiplication.

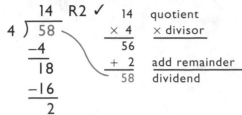

The answer 14 R2 is correct.

See *inverse, inverse operation.*

chord

A line joining two points on a circle.

Examples:

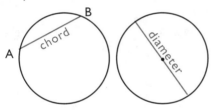

The diameter is the longest chord in a circle.

See *circumference, diameter.*

chronological order

Events arranged by the date or time when they happened. (See chart in next column.)

Example: The history of π

Time	Who/Where	Value of π
2000 BC	Babylonia	$3\frac{1}{8}$
300 BC	Archimedes	$3\frac{10}{71}$ to $3\frac{1}{7}$
AD 1220	Fibonacci	3.141 818
1665	Newton	3.141 592 653 589 7932
1705		π sign was first used
1949	ENIAC computer	π correct to 2035 decimal places
1984	Tokyo	π computed to 16 million decimal places

See *pi, time line.*

circle

The set of all points in a plane that are at the same distance (radius r) from a given point O (center).

Example:

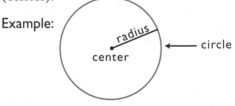

See *center, circumference, diameter, plane, radius of a circle.*

circle graph

See *pie chart.*

circumference

The distance around a circle.

If the radius is r units, then the circumference C is $2\pi r$ units.

$$C = 2\pi r$$

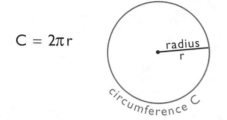

When the diameter d is measured, then the circumference C is πd units.

$$C = \pi d$$

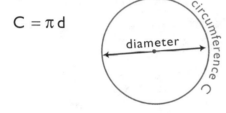

See *circle, diameter, pi (π)*.

class

A group, set, or a collection of things.

Example:

Triangles, squares, rectangles, and kites belong to the class of polygons.

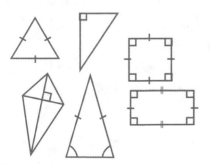

See *classification, classify, collection.*

classification

Arrangement into classes, sets, or groups, according to attributes.

Examples:

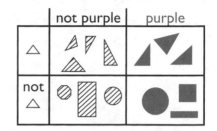

	Have pets	Don't have pets
	Quong	Halima
	Kelly	Nick
	Grant	Dean
	Toula	Anna
	Ali	Scott
	Claire	Sachiko

See *attribute, property.*

classify

Sort objects, ideas, or events into groups, classes, or hierarchies according to one or more properties or attributes.

See *attribute, property, sorting.*

clockwise

The direction in which the hands of a clock normally travel.

Example:

start

2:00   2:25

The hands on this clock have moved in a clockwise direction.

Screws and bottle tops are tightened clockwise.

See *counterclockwise.*

closed curve

A curve that starts at a point and comes back to that point.

Examples:

(i) simple closed curves

(ii) closed curves that are not simple

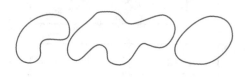

(iii) regular closed curves

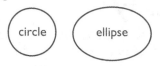

See *circle, curve, ellipse, open curve.*

closed shape

A shape (polygon) whose sides begin and end at the same point.

Examples:

closed shapes

These are not closed shapes.

See *polygon, shape.*

cm

A symbol for centimeter.

See *centimeter, symbol.*

code

A system of words, letters, or symbols which represent other letters, words or sentences. Codes are used for secret writing or signaling.

Example: Morse code

/— —/— — —/ — /• • • •/•/• — •/
M   O   T   H   E   R

coefficient

The number (constant term) in front of a variable in an algebraic term.

Examples:

$3y$	3 is the coefficient of y.
$7(a+b)$	7 is the coefficient of $(a+b)$.
xy	The coefficient is 1.

See *algebra.*

cointerior angles

See *parallel lines.*

collinear

Three or more points that lie on the same straight line.

A, B, C and D are collinear points

See *line, point.*

column

A vertical arrangement.

Examples:

13	
5	
18	
27	
9	
column of numbers	column of cars

See *column graph.*

combination

A way of arranging the objects in a group. The order of the objects does not matter.

Example:

There are four shapes in this group.

○ □ △ ⬡

Some possible combinations are:

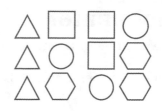

See *permutation.*

combined shapes
(complex)

Plane shapes that are made of two or more polygons.

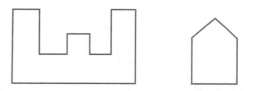

To calculate the area of a combined shape, divide it into simple shapes, find the area of each shape, then add the areas to find the area of the combined shape.

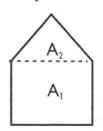

$$\text{Area} = A_1 + A_2$$

common denominator

For two or more fractions, a number that is a common multiple of the denominators.

Example:
For the fractions $\frac{1}{2}$ and $\frac{1}{3}$ a common denominator is 6, and also 12, 18, 24, etc.

See *denominator, fraction, least common denominator.*

common fraction

See *simple fraction.*

commutative property of addition

The order in which two or more numbers are added does not affect the answer (sum).

Example:
$$6 + 4 \;=\; 4 + 6$$
$$10 \;=\; 10$$

See *associative property of addition, sum.*

commutative property of multiplication

The order in which two or more numbers are multiplied does not affect the answer (product).

Example:
$$3 \times 8 \;=\; 8 \times 3$$
$$24 \;=\; 24$$

See *associative property of multiplication, product.*

comparison

Identifying whether objects, measures, or quantities are the same or different.

Examples:

same objects   different objects

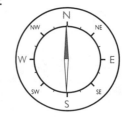

same heights   different heights

See *division, ratio.*

compass

An instrument that shows direction. Used in ships, airplanes, etc.

Example:

See *bearing, direction.*

compass

An instrument used to draw a circle and to mark off equal lengths.

complement

Something that completes or fills up a whole.

See *complementary addition, complementary angles.*

complementary addition

(i) Finding the amount to complete a set.

Example:
What has to be added to seven to make ten?

$7 + \square = 10$

$7 + 3 \;\;= 10$

Answer: Three has to be added.

(ii) Counting on to a higher total (as change is given after a purchase).

Example:
Shopping costs $17.50. I pay with a $20 bill. I get $2.50 change. This is evaluated by finding what must be added to $17.50 to make $20.

(iii) The method of "subtracting" that converts the subtraction question to an addition question.

Example:
$21 - 19 = 2$

Instead of taking nineteen away from twenty-one we think how much must be added to nineteen to make twenty-one.

See *addition, set, subtraction.*

complementary angles

Two angles for which the sum of their measures is 90°.

Example:

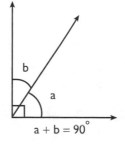

$a + b = 90°$

∠a and ∠b are complementary.

∠a is the complement of ∠b.

∠b is the complement of ∠a.

See *supplementary angles.*

complex fraction

A fraction whose numerator, denominator, or both, are fractions.

Examples:

$$\frac{\frac{1}{2}}{5} \qquad \frac{3}{\frac{4}{7}} \qquad \frac{\frac{1}{2}}{\frac{3}{4}} \qquad \frac{\frac{a}{b}}{\frac{c}{d}}$$

Note: To simplify a complex fraction, think of the bar as a division sign and divide as you would with fractions.

Simplify $\dfrac{\frac{1}{2}}{\frac{2}{3}}$.

$$\frac{1}{2} \div \frac{2}{3} = \frac{1}{2} \times \frac{3}{2} = \frac{3}{4}$$

composite number

A number with factors other than itself and one.

Examples:

12 = 12 × 1 or 3 × 4 or 6 × 2

33 = 33 × 1 or 3 × 11

Both twelve and thirty-three are composite numbers.

17 = 17 × 1   23 = 23 × 1

Seventeen and twenty-three are not composite numbers.

Numbers like seventeen which have no other factors except themselves and one are called prime numbers.

Every whole number greater than one is either:

(i)   a prime number
      (2, 3, 5, 7, 11 ...)
or
(ii) a composite number
      (4, 6, 8, 9, 10, 12, 14 ...)

See *factors, prime number.*

computation

Using addition, subtraction, multiplication and/or division to find the answer. These operations can be performed mentally, in writing, or with the help of calculating aids such as calculators or computers.

See *abacus, calculator, computer, table.*

compute

To work out or calculate.

Example:

$$\begin{array}{r} {}^{1}3.2\,1 \\ \times\ {}^{1}4.7 \\ \hline 2\,2\,4\,7 \\ 1\,2\,8\,4 \\ \hline 1\,5\,0\,8\,7 \end{array}$$

concave

A shape that is hollowed or rounded inward like the inside of a bowl.

Examples:

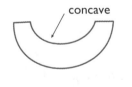
concave

concave lens

See *convex.*

concentric circles

Circles that are in the same plane and have the same center are concentric.

Example:

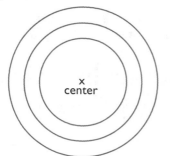

center

See *annulus, circle, plane.*

concurrent lines

Lines that intersect at the same point.

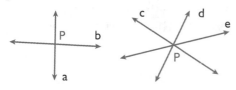

See *intersect, parallel lines.*

cone

A solid which has a circular base and comes in to a point at the top, similar in shape to an ice-cream cone.

Examples:

See *right 3D shape, solid.*

congruent

(Symbol: ≅)

Exactly equal. Matching exactly. Two figures are congruent if they have the same shape and the same size.

Examples:

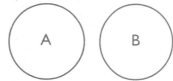

Circle A is congruent to circle B.

$$A \cong B$$

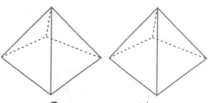

Congruent pyramids

See *corresponding angles, similar.*

conic section

A figure (ellipse, parabola, or hyperbola) formed when a right circular cone is cut by a plane.

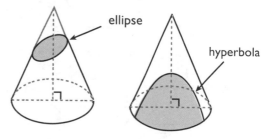

See *ellipse.*

consecutive numbers

Numbers that follow each other in a sequence.

Examples:

1 2 3 4 5 6 7 8 ...

$\dfrac{1}{7}$　$\dfrac{2}{7}$　$\dfrac{3}{7}$　$\dfrac{4}{7}$　$\dfrac{5}{7}$　$\dfrac{6}{7}$ ...

0.1　0.2　0.3　0.4 ...

See *sequence*.

conservation of area

Retaining the same area.

Examples:

(i)　The three triangles have the same area
$A = \frac{1}{2} \times 2$ cm $\times 2.5$ cm $= 2.5$ cm², even though their shapes are different.

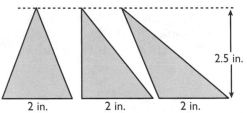

2.5 in.

2 in.　　2 in.　　2 in.

(ii)　The three shapes have the same area of 3 in.².

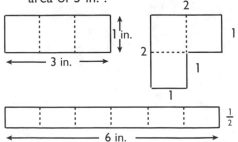

1 in.

3 in.

2

2

1

1

1

6 in.

$\frac{1}{2}$

See *area*.

constant

A symbol that always has the same value.

Example:

$2c + 6$

6 is a constant.

converging lines

Two or more lines that meet at the same point.

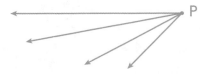

P

See *perspective*.

convex

Shaped like the outside of a circle or a sphere. The opposite of concave.

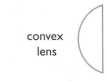

convex lens

See *concave*.

coordinates

A pair of numbers or letters that show the position of a point on the plane. The first number is always the x-coordinate, the second is the y-coordinate.

Examples:

(i)　Each point on the plane is given an ordered pair of numbers, written in parentheses.

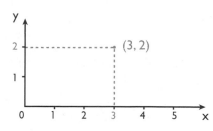

Point (3, 2) has the
x-coordinate 3, and the
y-coordinate 2.

(ii) The location of Laura Street is
D3.

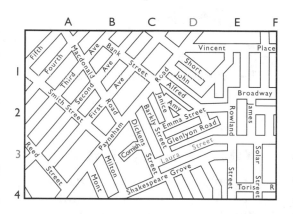

See *axis, intersection, ordered pair, origin.*

coplanar

Lying or being in the same plane.

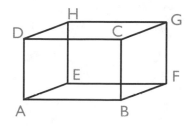

C, D, G and H are coplanar points.
AB and CG are not coplanar.

correspondence

See *one-to-one correspondence,
many-to-one correspondence.*

corresponding angles

Angles in the same or similar
position. In congruent shapes,
corresponding angles have the
same size (are congruent).

Example:

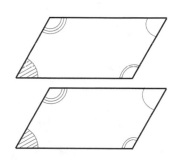

These parallelograms are congruent.
Corresponding angles are marked by the
same symbol.

See *congruent, parallel lines, vertically
opposite.*

corresponding sides

In congruent shapes, like the
triangles below, the sides AB and
XY, BC and YZ, and CA and ZX are
corresponding sides.

Example:

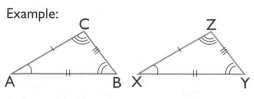

See *congruent.*

cost

The price of something.

counterclockwise

The direction opposite to that in which the hands of a clock travel.

Examples

9:30

This clock is fifteen minutes fast. The hands must be moved back to show the exact time.

9:15

The hands have been moved in a counterclockwise direction.

Screws and bottle tops are loosened in a counterclockwise direction.

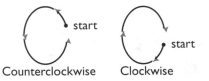

Counterclockwise   Clockwise

See *clockwise.*

counting

Giving one number to every item in a set. These numbers are in a sequence.

Example:

The numbers 1, 2, 3, 4, 5 ... are counting numbers.

See *cardinal number, sequence, set.*

counting number

A member of the set of numbers used in counting: {1, 2, 3, 4 ...} Note: zero is not a counting number.

See *cardinal number, number.*

counting system

A way of finding out how many objects there are.

See *decimal place-value system.*

cross-section of a solid

The face that is made when a solid is cut through by a plane.

Example:

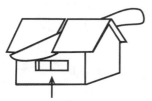

If you cut a house in half like this,

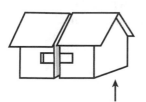

and took away this half,

then looking from here,

you would see this cross-section.

See *face, front view, plan, plane, side view.*

cube

A solid, shaped like a box, with twelve equal edges, six equal square faces and eight corners. A cube is a type of cuboid.

Examples:

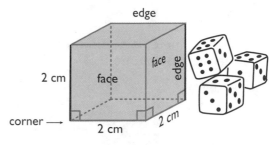

This is a diagram of a 2 cm cube.

See *cuboid, face, solid.*

cubed number

$$4^3 \leftarrow \text{exponent}$$

↑
base

4^3 means $4 \times 4 \times 4$ or 64.
We read it as *4 cubed,* or *4 to the third power.*

See *index, power of a number, square number.*

cubic centimeter

(Symbol: cm³)

A cubic centimeter is a unit for measuring volume.

Example:

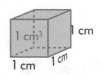

It is a cube with edges of 1 cm.

1 cm³ has a capacity of 1 milliliter.

See *capacity, cube, unit of measurement, volume.*

cubic meter

(Symbol: m³)

A cubic meter is a unit for measuring volume.

Example:

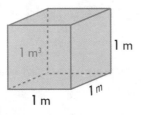

A cube whose edges are 1 meter long has a volume of 1 cubic meter.

$1 m^3 = 1,000,000 cm^3$

1 m³ has a capacity of 1 kiloliter.

See *capacity, unit of measurement, volume.*

cubic unit

A measure of volume.

See *cubic centimeter, cubic meter, volume.*

cuboid

A shape such as a shoe box. A cube-like prism. It has twelve edges, six faces and eight corners. The opposite faces are the same shape and size.

Examples:

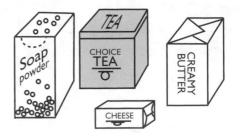

These boxes are cuboids.

See *cube, face, prism.*

curve

A line of which no part is straight. There are open curves and closed curves.

Examples:

open curves

closed curves

See *closed curve, open curve.*

cycle

A system that repeats itself in time.

Example:

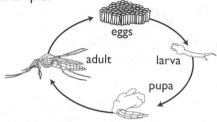

The breeding cycle of mosquitoes.

cylinder

A cylinder is a shape like a can. It is a solid with two circular faces at right angles to a curved surface.

Examples:

See *capacity, graduated, right 3D shape.*

data

A general term used to describe a collection of facts, numbers, measurements or symbols.

Example:

Students' scores in a math test were 15, 16, 18, 19, 19, 20, 21, 21, 22.

date

Specified time: day, month or year, at which something takes place.

Example:

The date on my letter was May 10, 1998.

day

The 24-hour period it takes the earth to turn once on its axis.

days of the week

Weekdays are: Monday, Tuesday, Wednesday, Thursday, and Friday. Weekend days are: Saturday and Sunday.

decade

Ten years.

decagon

A polygon with ten sides.

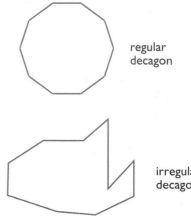

regular decagon

irregular decagon

See *polygon.*

decahedron

A polyhedron with ten faces.

Example:

This decahedron has been made by joining two pyramids and cutting their tops off.

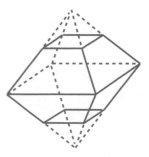

See *frustum, polyhedron.*

decimal

A number containing a decimal point. 0.07 and 1.35 are decimals.

decimal fraction

A fraction written as a decimal.

Example:

$$\frac{1}{10} = 0.1$$

fraction   decimal fraction

See *decimal place-value system.*

decimal place-value system

A numeration system with ten as a base for grouping. Commonly called the base ten system.

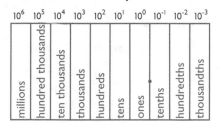

10^6	10^5	10^4	10^3	10^2	10^1	10^0	10^{-1}	10^{-2}	10^{-3}
millions	hundred thousands	ten thousands	thousands	hundreds	tens	ones	tenths	hundredths	thousandths

See *base, decimal point, place value.*

decimal point

A point that separates a decimal fraction from the whole number.

Example: 32.4

↑

decimal point

↓

7.62

See *point.*

decimal system

See *decimal place-value system.*

declination

The slope indicating where an object is compared to a vertical or horizontal position.

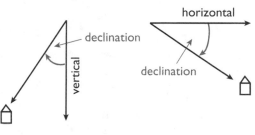

decrease

Make smaller. We either subtract a number or divide by a number.

Examples:
(i) Decrease this length by 2 cm.

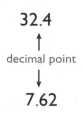

5 cm − 2 cm = 3 cm

We decreased 5 cm to 3 cm by cutting 2 cm off.

(ii) Decrease $100 five times.

$100 ÷ 5 = $20

$100 decreased five times is $20.

See *increase, progression.*

degree

(Symbol: °)

(i) In geometry, a degree is a unit for measuring angles.

Examples:

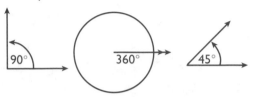

1 degree is divided into 60 minutes.
1° (degree) = 60′ (minutes)
1 minute is divided into 60 seconds.
1′ (minute) = 60″ (seconds)

(Don't confuse this with the symbols for feet and inches.)

(ii) The unit for measuring temperature.

See *angle, degree Celsius, geometry, temperature, unit of measurement.*

degree Celsius

(Symbol: °C)

In the metric system, the common unit for measuring temperature.

Example: The boiling point of water is 100°C. The freezing point of water is 0°C.

(The old unit was called degree Centigrade.)

See *temperature, thermometer.*

degree Fahrenheit

(Symbol: °F)

In the customary system, the common unit for

measuring temperature.

The boiling point of water is 212°F.
The freezing point of water is 0°F.

denominator

The number written below the line in a fraction; it tells how many parts there are in the whole.

Example:
This circle has been divided into 6 equal parts.

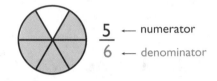

$$\frac{5}{6}$$ ← numerator
    ← denominator

In $\frac{5}{6}$ the denominator is 6.

See *fraction, numerator.*

density

(i) The compactness of a material.

(ii) The mass per unit of volume of a material. The relationship of mass to volume. Usually expressed as g/cm^3 or kg/m^3.

Example:
The density of water at 4°C is $1 g/cm^3$ (one gram per cubic centimeter).

depth

How deep something is. Measurement from the top down, from the front to the back or from the surface inwards.

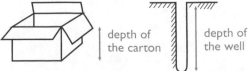

depth of the carton

depth of the well

descending order

Decreasing in value.

Example:
The following lengths have been arranged in descending order:

5.7 ft   4.9 ft   3.8 ft   1.25 ft
↑   ↑
longest   shortest

See *ascending order, decrease.*

diagonal

A line segment joining two corners that are not next to each other in any polygon.

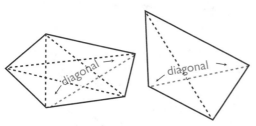

The dotted lines are diagonals.
See *polygon.*

diagram

A name given to pictures or sketches of geometric figures. It is also used for simplified drawings which explain or describe other things.

Examples:

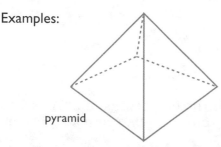

pyramid

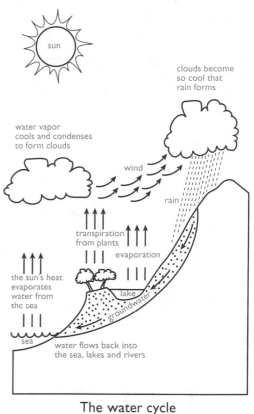

The water cycle

diameter

A line segment joining two points of a circle and passing through the center of the circle. A diameter equals two radii (r).

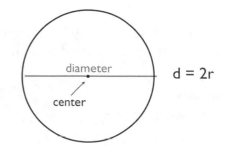

$d = 2r$

See *chord, circle, circumference, line segment, radius.*

diamond

A two-dimensional shape with four equal sides where the angles are not right angles.
The mathematical name is rhombus.

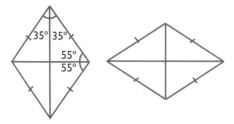

See *dimension, rhombus.*

difference

The amount by which two numbers differ.

Example:

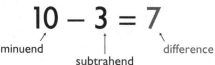

The difference between ten and three is seven.

See *minuend, subtract, subtraction, subtrahend.*

digit

Numerals 0, 1, 2, 3, ... 9 are called digits; we also call them one-digit numbers.

Examples:

4 is a one-digit number

56 is a two-digit number

813 is a three-digit number

See *place holder, place value.*

digital clock

A clock or a watch that shows time by numbers. It has no clock hands.

Example:

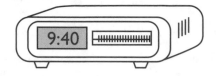

This clock shows twenty to ten.

See *a.m., analog clock, p.m., time interval.*

dimension

A property that can be measured, related to plane and space.

(i)　One-dimensional (1D) objects have only length.

Examples: lines, curves

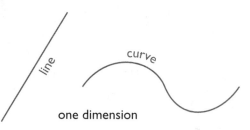

one dimension

(ii)　Two-dimensional (2D) objects have length and width.

Examples: plane figures–polygons, circles

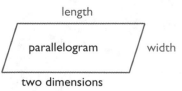

two dimensions

(iii) Three-dimensional (3D) objects have length, width, and height.

Examples: solids—cubes, pyramids

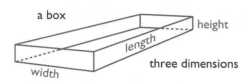

a box
height
length
width
three dimensions

Note: A point (dot) has no dimensions.

See *one-dimensional, plane, space, three-dimensional, two-dimensional.*

direct proportion

See *proportion.*

directed angle

The amount of turning from one ray (or arm of an angle) to the next, used in taking bearings.

Example:

N

N 40° E

40°

The directed angle (bearing) is N 40° E.
See *arm of angle, bearing.*

directed numbers

Numbers that have + or − signs. They are also called integers. We can show them on a number line.

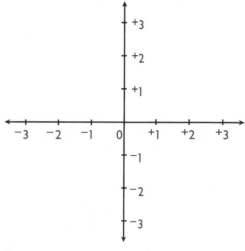

See *integers.*

direction

(i) The way to go.

Examples:
Left, right, up, down, above, below, inside, outside, near, from behind, forward, backward, etc.

(ii) Compass directions:

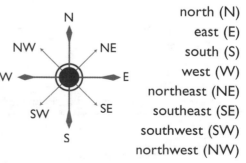

N
NW   NE
W   E
SW   SE
S

north (N)
east (E)
south (S)
west (W)
northeast (NE)
southeast (SE)
southwest (SW)
northwest (NW)

See *counterclockwise, clockwise, compass.*

displacement

A change in the position of an object or of a quantity of material.

Example:

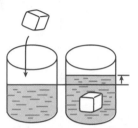

The quantity of water displaced by an immersed object.

The water displacement method is used to measure the volume of objects. The volume of displaced water is equal to the volume of the object.

See *volume*.

distance

The length between one point and another.

Example:

| |
4 in.

Distance between the points of the compass is 4 in.

Distance from my house to town is three miles.

3 mi

distribute

Give a share of something to each; deal out as in division.

Nan is going to distribute the cakes.

See *division*.

distribution

See *frequency distribution*.

distributive property

$$a\,(b + c) = ab + ac$$

Every term inside the grouping symbols is multiplied by the term that is immediately outside. The product of a factor and a sum is equal to the sum of the products.

See *expand, expanded notation, grouping symbols*.

dividend

A number that is to be divided by another number.

Example:

$$24 \div 6 = 4$$

dividend　　divisor　　quotient

24 is the dividend.

See *divisor, quotient*.

divisibility tests

A number is divisible by another if, after dividing, there is no remainder.

A number is

Divisible by	If	Examples
2	the last digit is even	2, 4, 6, ... 122 ...358 ...1000
3	the sum of all digits can be divided by 3	261 2+6+1=9 3672 3+6+7+2=18 18 1+8=9
4	the last two digits are divisible by 4	1,024 24 ÷ 4 = 6
5	the last digit is 5 or 0	15, 70...
7	there is no divisibility test	
8	the last 3 digits are divisible by 8	75,384 384 ÷ 8 = 48
9	the sum of its digits is divisible by 9	3,123 3+1+2+3=9
10	the number ends in 0	10, 20, 30...

Important: **No number can be divided by 0.**

See *factors, remainder.*

divisible

A number is divisible by another number if, after dividing, there is no remainder.

Example:
$72 ÷ 9 = 8$ $72 ÷ 8 = 9$

Seventy-two is divisible by nine and also by eight.

Seventy-two is *not* divisible by seven.

See *factors, remainder.*

division

Division is a mathematical operation that can be interpreted in several different ways:

(i)   Grouping

Example:

How many groups of 3 can be made with 15 apples?

The apples are to be placed into groups of equal size, 3 to a group. The problem is to find out how many groups there will be.

$15 ÷ 3 = 5$

There are 5 groups of 3 apples.

Repeated subtraction is a form of grouping.

(ii) Sharing (partition)

Example:
Share 15 apples among 5 children. How many apples will each child get?

The apples are to be separated into 5 equal groups. The problem is to find how many there will be in each group.

$$15 \div 5 = 3$$

(iii) Ratio
Comparison between two quantities.

Example:

 to

$$10 : 100 = 1 : 10$$

10 mL   100 mL

Ratio 1 : 10

Mixing 1 part juice and 10 parts water to make a drink.

See *ratio*.

divisor

A number which is to be divided into another number.

Example:

$$24 \div 6 = 4$$

dividend   divisor   quotient

6 is the divisor.
See *dividend, quotient*.

dodecagon

A polygon with twelve sides.

Examples:

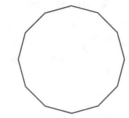

regular dodecagon

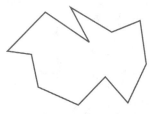

irregular dodecagon

See *polygon*.

dodecahedron

A solid (polyhedron) with twelve faces.
A regular dodecahedron is made by joining together twelve congruent regular pentagons.

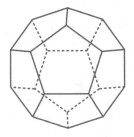

regular dodecahedron

See *pentagon, polyhedron, regular polyhedron*.

dollar

(Symbol: $)

A unit of money.
One dollar = 100 cents
         = 4 quarters
         = 10 dimes
         = 20 nickels

See *cent.*

dot paper

Paper printed with dots arranged in a pattern. It is used for drawing shapes, defining areas, games, etc., and to record work done on a geoboard.

Examples:

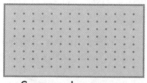

Square dot paper

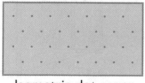

Isometric dot paper

See *geoboard, isometric graph paper, square paper.*

double

Twice as many, or the same again.

Examples:

is double

Double 8 is 16.

10 is double 5.

dozen

Twelve items.

Example:

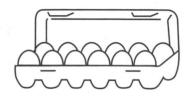

One dozen eggs = 12 eggs

edge

In geometry, the line that is the intersection of two plane faces.

Examples:

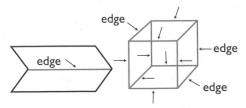

See *face, intersection, plane.*

element of a set

One of the individual objects that belong in (are members of) a set.

Example:

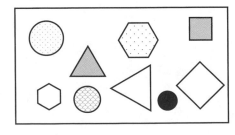

is an element of the set of shapes.

elevation, angle of

See *angle of elevation.*

ellipse

A closed curve that looks like an elongated circle.

Example:

See *closed curve.*

enlargement

Make bigger. Enlargement is the most commonly used transformation. It can be done in many ways: using a grid, rays, by pantograph or a photocopier.

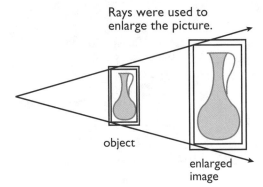

Rays were used to enlarge the picture.

object

enlarged image

See *pantograph, reduce, scale drawing, transformation.*

equal

(Symbol: $=$)

(i)   Identical in quantity.

Example:

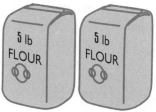

These two bags of flour have an equal weight of 5 lb.

(ii) Of the same value.

$1 bill equals four quarters.

(iii) $1 + 8, 3 + 6,$
      $10 - 1, 2 + 7,$
      $4 + 5$ and $9 + 0$
      are equal because they are all ways of representing 9.

See *equality, equal sign.*

equalizer

A balance with numbered hooks placed at intervals along the beam so that number facts can be represented, and equality indicated, by balance.

Example: A weight on the fifth hook on one side would balance weights on the second and third hooks on the other side.

$$5 \quad = \quad 2+3$$

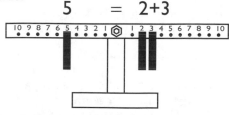

See *balance, equality.*

equality

The relation of being equal. A statement that two expressions are equal, usually expressed as an equation.

Example:

$$2 + 4 = 6$$

See *equal, equation, inequality.*

equally likely

Events that have the same chance of occurring are said to be equally likely.

Example:
When a die is rolled fairly, the six numbers, 1, 2, 3, 4, 5 and 6, are equally likely to occur.

See *chance event, probability.*

equal sign

(Symbol: $=$)

The name of the symbol that means "is equal to" or "equals." It shows that:

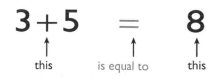

See *equal, symbol.*

equation

A statement that two quantities are equal. An equation has two sides which are equal or balanced. There must be the equal sign.

Example:

$x + 4 = 7$

This equation is true only if **x** has the value of three.

The **x** and any other signs or letters used in equations to stand for a quantity are called variables.

See *equality, inequality, variables.*

equilateral

Having sides of equal length.

(i) Square, regular pentagon, hexagon and other regular polygons have sides of equal length and angles of equal size.

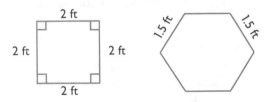

regular hexagon

(ii) equilateral triangle

A triangle that has three sides of equal length and three equal angles.

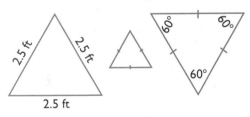

The angles of any equilateral triangle are always 60°.

See *triangle.*

equivalent

Having the same value. The same amount.

Example:

A quarter is equivalent to two dimes and a nickel.

See *equivalent fractions.*

equivalent fractions

Fractions that name the same amount.

Example:

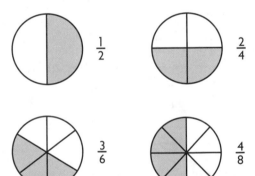

Fractions $\frac{1}{2}$, $\frac{2}{4}$, $\frac{3}{6}$, and $\frac{4}{8}$ are equivalent.

See *equivalent, fraction.*

estimate

(i) A rough or approximate calculation.

(ii) A number that has not been calculated accurately. Estimated answers are often needed when working with decimals.

Example:

For 1.9×3, you can estimate the product like this:

$$2 \times 3 = 6$$
$$1.9 \times 3 \approx 6$$

(iii) Trying to judge or guess what a measure or result will be.

Example:

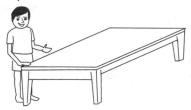

The table is about 6 feet long.

See *accurate, approximate, calculate, rounding.*

evaluate

To find the value of.

Examples:
(i) Evaluate 21×3.

$$\begin{array}{r} 21 \\ \times\ 3 \\ \hline 63 \end{array}$$

The value of 21×3 is 63.

(ii) Evaluate $p + 3q$

where $p = 2.5$ and $q = 7$

$$p + 3q = 2.5 + (3 \times 7)$$
$$= 2.5 + 21$$
$$= 23.5$$

even

Equally balanced, equal in number or amount.

Example:
$5 = $2.50 + $1 + $1.50

even number

A number that is divisible by two. All even numbers finish with one of the digits: 0, 2, 4, 6, or 8.

See *digit, divisible.*

exact

Precise, accurate, correct in every way, not approximate.

See *approximate.*

exchange

(i) When we go shopping, we exchange money for goods. Money is the medium of exchange.

Example:

$2.30 is the price of the toy car.

(ii) Base ten blocks can be exchanged.

Example:

ones   tens and ones

were exchanged for

16 ones 1 ten 6 ones

See *equivalent, base ten blocks.*

(iii) Money can also be exchanged for money of equivalent value.

Example:

is the same amount as

See *equivalent, base ten blocks, rate.*

expand

Write out in full.

Examples:

(i)

4

(ii) Expand 537

$$537 = 500 + 30 + 7$$

See *expanded notation.*

expanded notation

A way of writing numerals as a sum of the products of each digit and its place value.

Examples:

$249 = 200 + 40 + 9$

or $= (2 \times 100) + (4 \times 10) + (9 \times 1)$

or $= 2 \times 10^2 + 4 \times 10^1 + 9 \times 10^0$

exponent

A symbol indicating how many times the quantity is to be multiplied by itself to produce the power shown.

See *base, index, index notation, power of a number.*

expression

See *algebra*.

exterior

The outside of something.

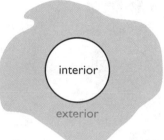

Examples:

(i) exterior angle

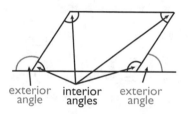

exterior   interior   exterior
angle   angles   angle

(ii) exterior angle of a triangle

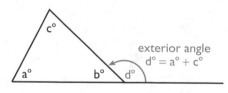

exterior angle
$d° = a° + c°$

The exterior angle of a triangle is the sum of the two opposite interior angles.

See *interior angles*.

face

In a three-dimensional shape, a face is the flat part of the surface that is bounded by the edges.

Examples:

(i) A cube has six faces.

(ii) A tetrahedron has four faces.

(iii) A pyramid has five faces.

See *cube, edge, plane shapes, pyramid, surface, tetrahedron, three-dimensional.*

factorization

We can simplify algebraic expressions by extracting a common factor.

Example: Factorize $3a + 6b$

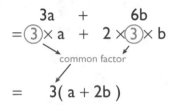

$$= 3(a + 2b)$$

See *algebraic expression.*

factors

All the whole numbers that can be divided exactly into a given number.

Examples: factor

(i) $6 \div 1 = 6$ 1
$6 \div 2 = 3$ 2
$6 \div 3 = 2$ 3
$6 \div 6 = 1$ 6

1, 2, 3 and 6 are factors of 6.

(ii) $5 \div 1 = 5$
$5 \div 5 = 1$

Prime number 5 has only the factors 5 and 1.

See *composite number, factor tree, prime number, whole number.*

factor tree

A diagram that shows the prime factors of a given number.

Example:

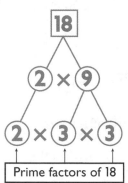

See *prime factor of a number.*

false sentence

A number sentence that is not true.

Examples:
5 < 1 is a false sentence.

The open sentence 3 + □ = 10 becomes false, if □ is replaced by any other number than 7, e.g. 3, 4, 5 ...

If □ is replaced by 7, it will become a true sentence.

See *number sentence, true sentence.*

farthest

The longest distance away.

Example:

Name	Distance
Kate	3.50 m
Paul	3.89 m
Mike	3.47 m

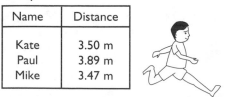

Paul jumped the farthest.
See *distance.*

figure

Another name for a numeral, line, shape, or solid.

Examples:
(i)   Write in figures: thirty-six **36**

(ii) Half of this figure has been colored in.

finite

Anything that has boundaries or can be counted.

Examples:
(i)   The region inside a square is finite because it is bounded by a perimeter.

(ii) The set of months in a year is a finite set because the months can be counted.

See *infinite, perimeter, region, set.*

first

The one at the beginning, before any other.

Example:

The first shape is a square.

flat

Being in one plane only.

Every face of a
cube is flat.

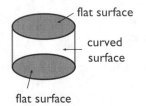

See *cube, face, plane, surface.*

flexible

A jointed structure is flexible when
its angles can be changed by
moving the sides.

Example:

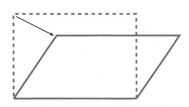

A rectangle is a flexible structure.
See *rigid.*

flip

A move of a figure over a line. The
resulting figure is like a mirror
image.

See *reflection, slide, turn.*

foot

(Plural: feet)
(Symbols: ′ , ft)

A measure of length.
1 foot = 12 inches
1 foot ≈ 30 centimeters

formula

An equation that uses symbols to
represent a statement.

Example:

Statement: The area of a rectangle is
found when its length is multiplied by
its width.

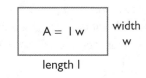

Formula:
$A = l \times w$
See *area, equation, symbol.*

fraction

A number that compares part of an object or a set with the whole.

Examples:

(i) The fraction $\frac{3}{4}$ means 3 parts out of a total of 4 equal parts.

$\frac{3}{4}$

3 parts out of 4 parts are shaded

(ii) 7 parts out of 100 parts are shaded.

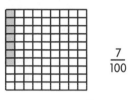

$\frac{7}{100}$

The fraction is $\frac{7}{100}$.

(iii) Shade $\frac{3}{4}$ of 8.

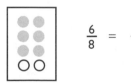

$\frac{6}{8} = \frac{3}{4}$

See *equivalent fraction, improper fraction, mixed number, proper fraction, simple fraction.*

frequency

The number of times an item occurs in a set of data.

Example:

We tossed a die 50 times and recorded the number for each throw.

We kept a tally of the 50 scores.

Number	Tally	Frequency
1	卌 II	7
2	卌 卌 II	12
3	卌 IIII	9
4	卌 III	8
5	卌 I	6
6	卌 III	8

Number 2 had the highest frequency.

Number 5 had the lowest frequency.

See *data, frequency distribution, tally.*

frequency distribution

A graph or table showing how often an event or quantity occurs.

Example:

A Frequency Distribution Table of Marks:

Mark	Tally	Frequency
20–29	I	1
30–39	卌	5
40–49	卌 IIII	9
50–59	卌 III	8
60–69	卌	5
70–79	III	3
80–89	I	1
	Total	32

frequency table

See *frequency distribution.*

front view

A diagram of an object, as seen from directly in front of it.

Example:

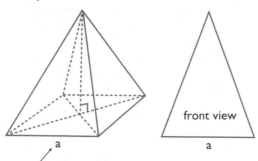

front view

See *cross-section, plan, side view.*

frustum

A pyramid cut by a plane parallel to the pyramid's base.

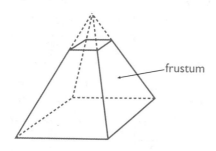

frustum

See *decahedron, pyramid, section.*

function

A set of ordered pairs in which no two pairs have the same x-coordinate.

g

(i)   g is the symbol for gram.

(ii) It is also a symbol for gravity. The force of gravity on the earth's surface is 1 g.

See *mass, newton, weight.*

geoboard

A board studded with nails forming a pattern or grid, usually of squares or equilateral triangles. Geoboards are used for shape and number activities in which elastic bands are arranged around sets of nails.

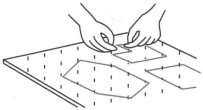

See *equilateral triangle, grid, pattern.*

geometric progression

See *progression.*

geometry

The part of mathematics that deals with the relationships, properties and measurements of solids, surfaces, lines, angles and space.

See *measure, property, solid, space, surface.*

Goldbach's conjecture

Every even integer greater than 2 is equal to the sum of two prime numbers.

$4 = 2 + 2$ $12 = 5 + 7$

$6 = 3 + 3$ $14 = 7 + 7$

$8 = 5 + 3$ $24 = 11 + 13$

$10 = 3 + 7$ $42 = 19 + 23$

See *natural numbers, prime numbers.*

googol

A very large number. It has the numeral 1 with one hundred zeros after it.

1,000,000,000,000,000,000,000
000,000,000,000,000,000,000
000,000,000,000,0 ...

gradient

Measurement of slope, inclination to horizontal, or the pitch. It is measured and expressed as a ratio.

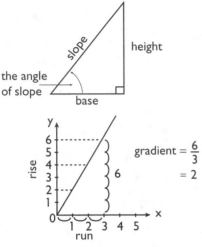

The ratio $\frac{\text{height}}{\text{base}}$ or $\frac{\text{rise}}{\text{run}}$ is called the slope, the gradient, or the pitch.

graduated

Marked off with measurements.

Examples:

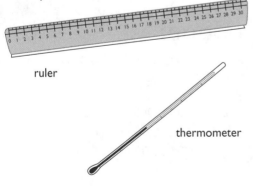

ruler

thermometer

A thermometer is graduated in degrees.

A ruler is graduated in centimeters or inches.

gram
(Symbol: g)

A unit of mass.
1,000 g = 1 kg

Examples:

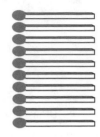

The mass of this box of chocolates is 250 grams.

The mass of ten matches is approximately 1 gram.

See *mass, unit of measurement.*

graph

Drawings or diagrams that show information, usually about how many things.

See *bar graph, histogram, line graph, pictograph, pie chart.*

greater than
(Symbol: >)

A relation between a pair of numbers showing which is greater.

Example:

$$7 > 6$$

greater than

See *less than.*

greatest common factor
(GCF)

The greatest number that divides into all given numbers.

Example:

For given numbers 8, 12, 16 and 20 the greatest common factor (GCF) is 4.

See *factors, factor tree.*

grid

Regular lines that go across, up and down. Often found on maps and graphs.

Examples:

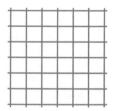

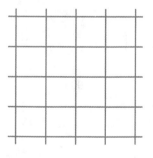

See *isometric paper, square paper.*

gross

Twelve dozen, 144.

group

(i) Putting things together in a set or group. In the decimal system things are grouped into tens.

Hundreds	Tens	Ones
2	4	3

243 = 2 groups of 100
 4 groups of 10
 3 groups of 1

(ii) Two or more things.

A group of boys.

See *grouping.*

grouping

Putting things together into sets with the same number in each set.

Example:

How many groups of four can be made with twenty balls?

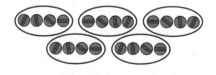

Answer: Twenty balls are put into five groups of four.

See *division, set.*

grouping symbols

See *brackets.*

h

Symbol for height, hour.

ha

A symbol for hectare.

half

(Plural: halves)

One part of two equal parts.

Examples:

(i)

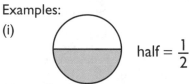

$$\text{half} = \frac{1}{2}$$

(ii) Half of twenty-four is twelve.

$$\frac{1}{2} \times 24 = 12$$

(iii) An orange has been cut into two halves

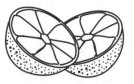

handspan

The distance from the top of the thumb to the top of the smallest finger when the hand is fully stretched.

Example:

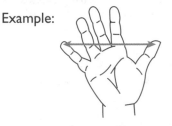

This is a handspan.

A handspan is used as an arbitrary measure for estimating the lengths, heights or widths of objects.

See *arbitrary unit, estimate.*

hectare

(Symbol: ha)

A unit of area.
One hectare is the area of a square with sides measuring 100 meters.

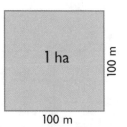

1 ha

100 m

100 m

The area of a soccer field is approximately half a hectare.

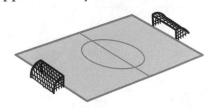

See *area, unit of measurement.*

heft

To judge the weight of objects by lifting them in the hands.

Examples:

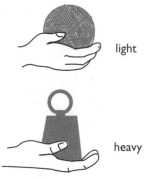

light

heavy

See *weight*.

hemisphere

Half of a sphere.

Example: Australia lies in the southern hemisphere.

Each part is $\frac{1}{2}$ of a sphere.

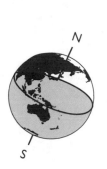

hemisphere

See *sphere*.

height

Measurement from top to bottom; the vertical distance.

Examples:

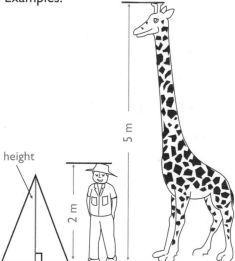

height

5 m

2 m

See *altitude, vertical*.

heptagon

A polygon with seven sides and seven angles. Regular heptagons have all sides congruent and all angles the same.

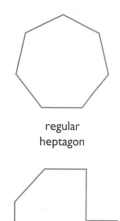

regular
heptagon

irregular
heptagon

See *polygon*.

hexagon

A shape (polygon) that has six sides and six angles.

Examples:

regular hexagon

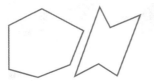

irregular hexagons

A honeycomb is made up of regular hexagons.

See *polygon*.

hexagram

A shape formed by two intersecting equilateral triangles.

hexahedron

A solid (polyhedron) with six faces. All cuboids are hexahedrons. A cube is a regular hexahedron; all six faces are congruent squares, all internal angles are equal.

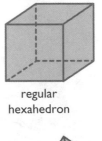

regular hexahedron

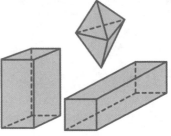

irregular hexahedrons

See *cube, cuboid, polyhedron, prism, regular polyhedron*.

Hindu–Arabic

Our system of numbers. It is the result of centuries of development.

The symbols for all the digits, except zero, probably originated with the Hindus in India, as early as 200 B.C.

Hindu numerals

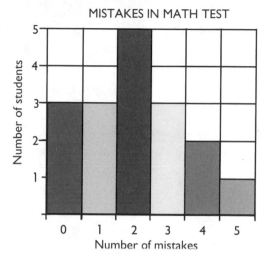

The Arabs adopted the system.
Arabic numerals (13th century
AD.)

^{0} l 2 3 4 5 6 7 8 9

The numerals, including zero, were
standardized after the invention of
the printing press in the 15th
century.

0 1 2 3 4 5 6 7 8 9

The modern system has very useful
characteristics:
1   It has only ten digits: 0, 1, 2, 3,
     4, ...9.
2   It uses zero as a placeholder.
3   It uses a place value system;
     the value of a digit depends on
     its placement in the numeral:
     37   307   13,700

See *numeral, place value.*

histogram

A bar graph with no spaces
between columns.

MISTAKES IN MATH TEST

See *column, column graph.*

horizon

Line at which land and sky appear
to meet.

See *horizontal line.*

horizontal line

Line parallel to, or on a level with, the horizon.

A vertical line is at right angles to the horizon.

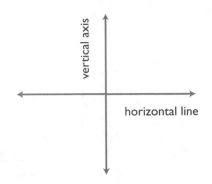

See *axis, bar graph, base line, parallel, right angle, vertical.*

horizontal surface

Any surface which is parallel to, or on a level with, the horizon.

Examples:

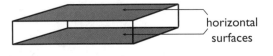

See *horizon, parallel, surface.*

hour

(Symbol: h)

A unit of time.

    1 hour = 60 minutes

    1 hour = 3,600 seconds

    24 hours = 1 day

See *unit of measurement..*

hypotenuse

The longest side of a right triangle (the side directly opposite the right angle).

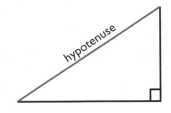

See *Pythagoras' theorem, right triangle.*

image

An exact copy of an object.

Example:

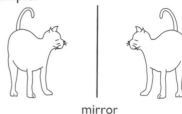

mirror

The image in a mirror.
See *mapping, mirror image, reflection.*

icosahedron

A solid (polyhedron) with twenty faces.
A regular icosahedron is formed by joining together twenty congruent equilateral triangles.

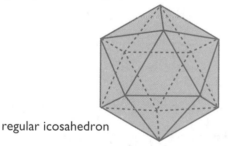

regular icosahedron

See *polyhedron, regular polyhedron.*

improper fraction

A fraction whose numerator is greater than its denominator.

Example:

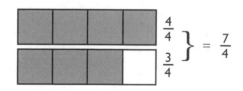

See *denominator, fraction, mixed number, numerator, proper fraction.*

identical

Exactly alike.

Examples:

5   5

inch

(Symbols: ", in.)

A measure of length.

12 inches = 1 foot

1 inch ≈ 2.5 cm

increase

Make larger by adding a certain amount, or multiplying by a number.

Examples:

(i) The price of a one dollar bus ticket has been increased by twenty cents.

$1 + 20c = $1.20

(ii) My family of 2 cats has increased 3 times. How many kittens do I have now?

2 x 3 = 6

6 − 2 = 4
I have 4 kittens.

See *decrease, progression.*

index

(Plural: indices)

5^3 index or exponent

base

Index is also called exponent.

In $\sqrt[3]{5}$ the index is 3. Where no index is written, as in $\sqrt{5}$, the index is 2.

See *base, exponent, index notation, square root.*

index laws

In algebra, when working with indices or algebraic expressions, these laws must be remembered:

Law:

$$x^a \times x^b = x^{a+b}$$

$$\frac{x^a}{x^b} = x^{a-b}$$

$$x^0 = 1$$

$$(x^a)^b = x^{a\times b} = x^{ab}$$

$$(x \times y)^a = x^a y^a$$

$$\left(\frac{x}{y}\right)^a = \frac{x^a}{y^a}$$

$$x^{-a} = \frac{1}{x^a}$$

$$\sqrt[n]{a} = a^{\frac{1}{n}}$$

Example:

$$5^3 \times 5^2 = 5^{3+2} = 5^5$$

$$\frac{5^3}{5^2} = 5^{3-2} = 5^1 = 5$$

$$5^0 = 1$$

$$(5^3)^2 = 5^{3\times2} = 5^6$$

$$(5 \times 4)^3 = 5^3 \times 4^3$$

$$\left(\frac{5}{4}\right)^3 = \frac{5^3}{4^3}$$

$$5^{-3} = \frac{1}{5^3}$$

$$\sqrt[3]{5} = 5^{\frac{1}{3}}$$

index notation

A shorthand way of writing large numbers such as 1,000,000. Also called scientific notation.
Using index notation:
1,000,000 = 10 × 10 × 10 × 10 × 10 × 10 = 10^6

10^6 index or exponent

base

is read as:
ten to the power of six or
ten to the sixth power.

See *base, cubed number, power of a number, scientific notation, square number.*

inequality

A statement that one quantity is less than or greater than another. The symbols $<$, $>$ and $\neq$ are used to express inequalities.

Examples:

$5 \neq 6$ Five is not equal to six.
$5 < 6$ Five is less than 6.
$6 > 4$ Six is greater than 4.

See *equality, greater than, less than, not equal.*

inequality signs

Sign:	Meaning:
$<$	less than
$\leq$	less than or equal to
$\neq$	not equal to
$>$	greater than
$\geq$	greater than or equal to

infer

Make a predictive statement or conclusion, based on observation or reasoning.

See *prediction.*

infinite

Without bounds of size or number, unlimited, not finite, endless.

Example:
The set of whole numbers is an infinite set.

See *finite, set, whole number.*

infinite decimal

(not terminating)

Decimals which go on without an end.

Example:
$\pi = 3.1415927...$

See *repeating decimal, terminating decimal.*

infinity

(Symbol: ∞)

Expressing quantity without bounds.

See *infinite.*

input

See *number machine.*

insignificant zeros

Unnecessary zeros in decimal numbers.

Example:

incorrect	correct
0̲5.2	5.2
9.980̲	9.98
.25	0.25

integers

Positive or negative whole numbers and zero.

Examples:

Integers

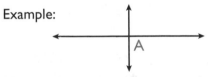

The set of integers:

$\{...-6, -5, -4, -3, -2, -1, 0, 1, 2, 3, 4, 5...\}$

See *directed, negative and positive numbers, set, whole number.*

intercept

When drawing graphs of equations, an intercept is the point where the equation line crosses an axis.

Example:

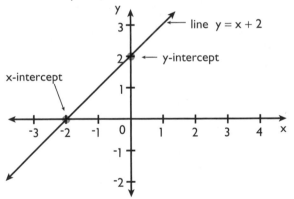

The line $y = x + 2$ crosses the y-axis at point $(0, 2)$. The point $(0, 2)$ is called the y-intercept.

The line also crosses the x-axis at point $(-2, 0)$, which is called the x-intercept.

See *coordinates, gradient.*

interior

The inside of something.

See *exterior.*

interior angles

Angles inside a shape.

Example:

The sum of the interior angles of any triangle is $180°$.

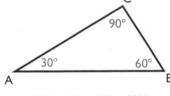

$30° + 60° + 90° = 180°$

intersect

To cut across. To cross each other.

Example:

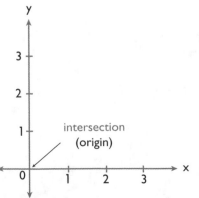

The two lines intersect at point A.

intersection

(i) The place where two or more lines meet, like an intersection of two streets.

(ii) The region where shapes overlap.

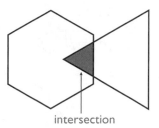

intersection

(iii) (Of sets) The set of elements that are common to both sets.

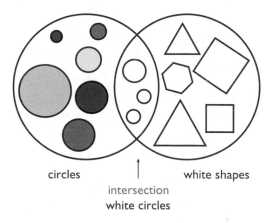

circles   white shapes

intersection
white circles

See *coordinates, origin, region, set, shape.*

interval

The amount of time, or distance, between two events or places.

Examples:

(i) There is a twenty-minute interval between the two films.

(ii) Line segment.

←———|——————|———→ line
        interval

See *line.*

inverse

Inverted in position, order or relation. When one quantity increases, the other decreases at the same rate.

See *additive inverse, proportion, ratio.*

inverse factor tree

A diagram that starts with prime numbers and works back to the number they are factors of.

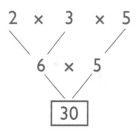

Prime numbers: 2, 3 and 5 have a product of 30.

See *factor tree, prime factor of a number.*

inverse operations

The operation which reverses the action of the original operation.

Examples:

Addition and subtraction are inverse operations.
4 + 3 = 7
7 − 3 = 4

Multiplication and division are inverse operations.
6 x 3 = 18
18 ÷ 3 = 6

See *operation, reciprocal.*

invert

Turn upside down, reverse position.

$\frac{1}{2}$ inverts to $\frac{2}{1}$

$\frac{3}{4}$ inverts to $\frac{4}{3}$

irrational numbers

Numbers that cannot be written as integers or ratios.
Examples:

$$\pi, \quad \sqrt{2}, \quad \sqrt{3}, \quad \sqrt[3]{2}$$

See *rational numbers*.

irregular polygon

A shape in which not all sides are equal in length, and/or at least one angle is different in size from the other angles.

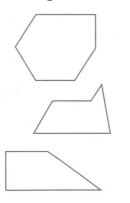

See *polygon, regular polygon*.

isometric drawing

A drawing where the three dimensions are represented by three sets of lines 120° apart, and all measurements are in the same scale (not in perspective).

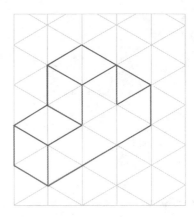

See *perspective*.

isometric graph paper

Paper with dots or lines that make equilateral triangles. Used for isometric drawings.

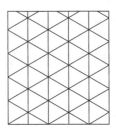

See *equilateral triangle, square paper*.

isosceles triangle

A triangle in which two sides have the same length and two angles have the same measure.

Examples:

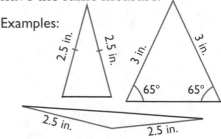

kilometer

(Symbol: km)

A unit of distance. Long distances are measured in kilometers.

1 km = 1,000 m

Example:

The road distance from Darwin to Katherine is 352 km.

See *distance, unit of measurement.*

kilogram

(Symbol: kg)

The base unit of mass.

1 kg = 1,000 g

Examples:
The mass of this bag of sugar is one kilogram.

The mass of this girl is twenty-seven kilograms.

See *gram, mass, unit of measurement.*

kite

A quadrilateral is shaped like this.

The two short sides are equal in length. The two long sides are equal in length. The diagonals are perpendicular to each other.

See *quadrilateral.*

kiloliter

(Symbol: kL)

A unit of volume (capacity) for measuring liquids.

1 kL = 1,000 L

Example:

Five 200-liter oil drums hold one kiloliter.

See *capacity, unit of measurement, volume.*

knot

(Symbol: kn)

The measure of speed at sea, equal to traveling one nautical mile per hour.

1 nautical mile = 1.852 kilometers

Example:

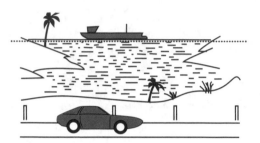

A ship moving at twenty knots is traveling as fast as a vehicle on land traveling about thirty-seven kilometers per hour.

L

(i) L is the symbol for liter.
(ii) In Roman numerals L stands
      for fifty.

See *capacity, liter.*

LCD

See *least common denominator.*

LCM

See *least common multiple.*

leap year

A year that has 366 days instead
of 365 days. It occurs every four
years.
In a leap year February has
twenty-nine days instead of
twenty-eight days.
When the year number can be
divided by 4 leaving no remainder,
then it is a leap year.

Examples:
$1979 \div 4 = 494 \text{ (r 3)}$
This is not a leap year.
$1980 \div 4 = 495$
This is a leap year.

Century years are not leap years
unless they are divisible by 400.

Example:
1600, 2000, 2400 are leap years.
1500, 1700, 1800 are not leap years.

least

The smallest thing or amount in a
group.

Example:

$3.50
$1.85
$5.20

The toy car costs the least amount.

least common denominator
(LCD)

The least counting number that is
divisible by the denominators of
given fractions. The least multiple
of two or more denominators.

Example:
What is the LCD of fractions $\frac{1}{4}$
and $\frac{1}{10}$?

4 divides exactly into   4, 8, 12, 16, (20), 24,
(Multiples of 4 are)   28, 32, (36), 40, 44....

10 divides exactly into   10, (20), 30, (40), 50,
(Multiples of 10 are)   60, 70....

The least number into which both 4 and 10 divide exactly is 20.

Therefore 20 is the LCD.
Least common denominators are used in addition and subtraction of fractions.

Example:

$$\frac{1}{4} + \frac{1}{10} = \frac{5}{20} + \frac{2}{20}$$
$$= \frac{7}{20}$$

See *common denominator, counting number, denominator, fraction, least common multiple.*

least common multiple
(LCM)

The least counting number that is a multiple of given numbers.

Example:

What is the LCM of 2 and 3?

The multiples of 2 are:

2, 4, ⑥, 8, 10, ⑫, 14, 16, ⑱ ...

The multiples of 3 are:

3, ⑥, 9, ⑫, 15, ⑱, 21, 24 ...

Common multiples are: 6, 12, 18 ...

The least common multiple of 2 and 3 is **6**.

See *counting number, multiple.*

length

How long something is from end to end.
(i)   The measure of distance.

Examples:

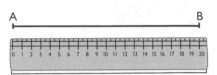

Line AB is twenty centimeters long.

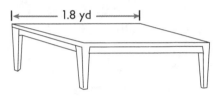

The length of this table is 1.8 yards.

(ii) An interval of time.

Example:
How long is the lunchtime break?

See *centimeter, distance, interval, kilometer, meter, millimeter.*

less than
(Symbol: <)

A relation between pairs of numbers showing which is less.

Example:

5 < 7

less than

See *greater than, inequality signs.*

like terms

Similar, resembling each other. In algebra, expressions are called like terms if they have the same variable and power. Like terms can be added and subtracted; terms that are not like cannot.

Examples:

Like terms	Unlike terms
$4x - 3x$	$a - b$
$5x^2y + x^2y$	$3x^2 + 3$

See *power, unlike terms, variable.*

line

A straight path of points that extends forever in both directions.

←——————————————→ a

A straight line is the shortest possible distance between two points.

See *curve, horizontal line, infinite, interval, line segment, vertical.*

linear

Involving measurement in one dimension only.

See *line.*

linear equation

An equation that can be presented as a straight line.

Examples:

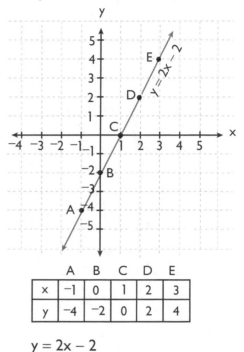

	A	B	C	D	E
x	−1	0	1	2	3
y	−4	−2	0	2	4

$$y = 2x - 2$$

See *equation.*

line graph

A graph formed by segments of straight lines that join the points representing certain data. Line graphs show changes over time.

Example:

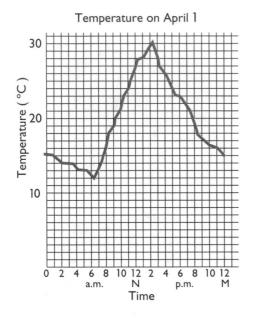

See *graph, line, line segment.*

line of symmetry

The line that divides something in half so that one half is the mirror image of the other half. This line is sometimes called an axis of symmetry.
A shape may have more than one line of symmetry.

Examples:

One line of
symmetry

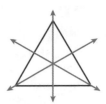

Three lines of
symmetry

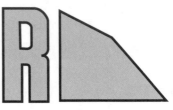

Some shapes have no
line of symmetry

See *asymmetry, axis, symmetry.*

line segment

Part of a straight line.

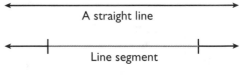

A straight line

Line segment

See *diameter, line.*

liter
(Symbol: L)

A unit of capacity used to measure the volume of liquids or the capacity of containers.

$$1 \text{ L} = 1,000 \text{ cm}^3 = 1,000 \text{ mL}$$

$$1,000 \text{ L} = 1 \text{ kL}$$

Example:

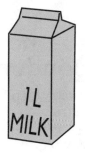

This carton of milk holds one liter.

See *capacity, unit of measurement, volume.*

magnitude

The size, or how big something is.

Example:

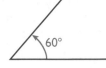

The magnitude of this angle is 60°.

See *directed numbers.*

m

(i)   m is the symbol for meter.
(ii) m is also the symbol for the prefix milli-.

M

(i)   M is the symbol for the prefix mega-, meaning one million.
(ii) In Roman numerals M means 1,000.

magic square

A puzzle where the numbers are arranged in a square so that each row, column and diagonal add up to the same total.

Example:

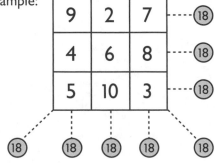

many-to-one correspondence

A match between members of two sets in which more than one element of the first set is associated with one element of the second. Arrows are used to show the relationship.

Example:

children and their favorite drinks

Three elements (Mary, Jane and Peter) of the first set are associated with one element (Cola) of the second set.

See *arrow diagram, one-to-one correspondence.*

mapping

A matching operation between two sets in which each member of the first set is assigned only one member of the second set as a partner or image.

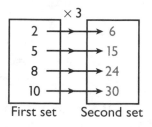

First set   Second set

In the above example, 2 maps onto 6, so 6 is the image of 2.

See *image, many to-one correspondence, one-to-one correspondence, set.*

mass

The amount of matter contained in an object.

Units of mass:

gram   g

kilogram   kg

tonne   t

1000 g = 1 kg

1000 kg = 1 t

Example:

This boy has a mass of twenty-eight kilograms.

See *beam balance, unit of measurement, weight.*

matching

See *many-to-one correspondence, one-to-one correspondence.*

mathematical shorthand

Instead of long sentences, mathematics uses numbers, symbols, formulas and diagrams.

Example:

The sentence,
"The area of a triangle is found when its base is multiplied by its perpendicular height and then divided by two,"
is written in mathematical shorthand as:

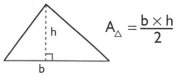

$$A_{\triangle} = \frac{b \times h}{2}$$

See *formula.*

maximum

The greatest or biggest value.

Examples:

1   The maximum temperature this month was 93° F.

2   The maximum speed is 50 kilometers per hour.

See *minimum.*

maze

A kind of puzzle in which a person has to find a way through a network of lines, paths, etc.

Example:

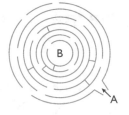

Follow the path from A to B without crossing any lines.

mean

The mean is the average of a set of numbers. It is found by adding all the numbers and then dividing the sum by the number of addends.

$$\text{Mean} = \frac{\text{sum of addends}}{\text{number of addends}}$$

See *average, measures of central tendency.*

measure

(i) To determine the size of something.

Examples:
How long? How tall? How heavy? How hot?

(ii) Compare quantities. A number assigned to a quantity that indicates its size compared to a chosen unit.

Example:

The length of the book is 10 in.

See *unit of measurement.*

measures of central tendency

The three measures are: mode, median, and mean. They usually fall in the middle of the distribution and tell us certain facts about it.

See *mean, median, mode.*

median

In statistics, the median is the middle number for an odd number of data, when numbers are arranged in order.

Example:

2, 2, 4, 5, 6, 8, 10
↑
median = 5

For an even number of data arranged in order, the mean is the average of the two middle numbers.

Example:

2, 3, 4, 8, 9, 10
∨
$$\text{median} = \frac{4+8}{2} = 6$$

See *average, mean, measures of central tendency, mode, score.*

megaliter

(Symbol: ML)

A unit of capacity.

1 megaliter = 1,000,000 liters

1 ML = 1,000,000 L

Example:
Volume (capacity) of this swimming pool is:

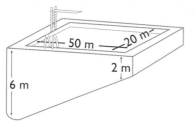

Volume = [50 × 20 × (6 − 2)] m³

= 4000 m³

= 4,000,000 L

= 4 ML

This swimming pool contains four megaliters (4 ML) of water.

meter

(Symbol: m)

The base unit of length (distance) in the metric system.

$$1 \text{ m} = 100 \text{ cm}$$
$$1 \text{ m} = 1,000 \text{ mm}$$

Example

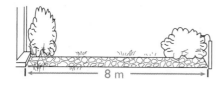

The path is eight meters long.

See *distance, unit.*

metric system

A decimal system of weights and measures. The base unit for length is meter, for mass is kilogram, and for time is second in the metric system.

See *decimal system, unit, basic, unit of measurement.*

midpoint

A point in the middle of an interval.

Example: $\overline{AM} = \overline{MB}$

The point M is the midpoint of the interval AB.

See *bisect, bisector.*

mile

A measure of length.
1 mile = 5,280 ft or 1,760 yd.

milligram

(Symbol: mg)

A very small unit of mass, used when working with medicines and chemicals. It is one-thousandth of a gram.

$$1 \text{ mg} = \frac{1}{1000} \text{ g}$$
$$1 \text{ mg} = 0.001 \text{ g}$$

See *gram.*

milliliter

(Symbol: mL)

A unit of capacity.

1,000 mL = 1 L

Note: One milliliter of water at four degrees Celsius has a mass of one gram.

A teaspoon holds 5 mL.

This bucket holds 12 L.

See *centimeter, volume.*

millimeter

(Symbol: mm)

A unit of length.

10 mm = 1 cm

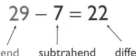

1 mm

0   10 mm   40   50

See *centimeter, length.*

million

One thousand thousands: 1,000,000.
See *billion.*

minimum

The smallest or least value.

Example:

The minimum temperature in July was 76° F.

See *maximum.*

minuend

A number from which another number is to be subtracted.

Example:

$$29 - 7 = 22$$

minuend   subtrahend   difference

29 is the minuend.

See *difference, subtract, subtrahend.*

minus

(Symbol: −)

Subtract or take away.

Example:

Eight minus two is written as $8 - 2$ and means two subtracted from eight.

$8 - 2 = 6$

See *subtract.*

minute

(Symbol: min)

(i)   A measure of time.
      One minute = sixty seconds
      1 min = 60 s

There are sixty minutes in one hour.

(ii) Angle measurement
      1 min = $\frac{1}{60}^{\circ}$ (degree)

1° (degree) = 60 min

mixed number

A whole number and a fraction.

Examples:

$1\frac{1}{2}$ $3\frac{5}{2}$

This is another way of writing an improper fraction:

$\frac{3}{2} = 1\frac{1}{2}$ $\frac{35}{30} = 1\frac{5}{30} = 1\frac{1}{6}$

See *fraction, improper fraction, whole number.*

möbius strip

A surface with only one side. It is made by giving a strip of paper or any other flexible material a half twist and then fastening the ends together.

If a line is drawn down the middle of the strip, it will come back to the starting point, having covered both sides of the strip, without the pencil being lifted.

Example:

A thin strip of paper...   can be given a twist...

and have the ends...   joined to make a möbius strip.

mode

In statistics, the number that occurs most often in a set of data.

Example:
For the set of data,
1, 1, 2, 4, 4, 6, 6, 6, 6, 7, 7, 7, 8, 10,

6 is the mode.

See *average, mean, measures of central tendency, median.*

model

A three-dimensional representation of an actual or designed object. It may be a physical structure, for example, a model of a cube made from cardboard.

Examples:

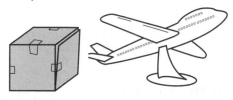

a model of   a model of
a cube   an airplane

See *net, scale drawing.*

month

A measure of time. There are twelve months in a year. The lengths of different months vary from twenty-eight to thirty-one days.
An easy way to remember the number of days in each month is to learn the following rhyme.

Thirty days has September,
April, June and November.
All the rest have thirty-one,
Except for February alone,
Which has but twenty-eight days clear,
And twenty-nine in each leap year.

See *calendar, day, leap year, year.*

more

Greater in amount.

Example:
Four dollars is more than three dollars.

most

The greatest amount.

Example:

Jim has twenty cents.
Betty has thirty-five cents.
Peter has thirty cents.
Betty has the most.

multilateral

Having many sides.

multiple

A multiple of a given number is any number into which it will divide exactly.

Examples:
Multiples of two are 2, 4, 6, 8, 10, 12 …
Multiples of three are 3, 6, 9, 12, 15, 18 …
Multiples of four are 4, 8, 12, 16, 20, 24 …

See *division, least common multiple.*

multiplicand

The number that is to be multiplied.

Example:

$$8 \times 7 = 56$$

multiplicand   multiplier   product

See *multiplication, multiplier, product.*

multiplication

(Symbol: $\times$)

Multiplication is repeated addition.

(i) 2 groups of 3,
    $2 \times 3 = 6$ or
(ii) 3 multiplied by 2,
    $3 \times 2 = 6$ or
(iii) 3 made 2 times bigger.

Sign $\times$ refers to two operations:
(i) groups of, and
(ii) multiplied by.

See *addition, operation.*

multiplication facts

See *table.*

multiplication property of one

When a number is multiplied by one, the product is equal to the original number. This is the multiplication property of one.

Examples:

$7 \times 1 = 7$

$1 \times 138 = 138$

Use of the property is made when a fraction is converted to an equivalent form.

Example:

$\frac{2}{3} = \frac{\square}{12}$

$\frac{2}{3} \times 1 = \frac{2}{3} \times \frac{4}{4}$

$\qquad = \frac{8}{12}$

$\frac{2}{3}$ has been multiplied by one

(or by $\frac{4}{4}$ which is equal to one)

multiplier

The number by which another number is multiplied.

Example:

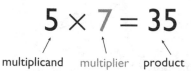

$5 \times 7 = 35$

multiplicand   multiplier   product

See *multiplicand, multiplication, product.*

multiply

Carry out the process of repeated addition or multiplication.

See *addition, multiplication.*

natural number

One of the counting numbers.

Examples:

1, 2, 3, 4, 5, 6, 7, 8, 9 ...

See counting number, positive numbers.

nautical mile

Used to measure travel at sea. One nautical mile equals 1,852 meters or 1.852 kilometers.

See knot.

negative number

A negative number is a number less than zero. Negative numbers are written with a negative sign (⁻) in front of them.

Examples:

⁻0.1, ⁻0.2, ... ⁻0.9, ... ⁻1, ⁻1.1, ...
⁻2, ... ⁻2.55 ...

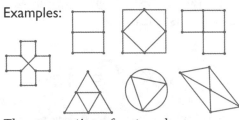

See integers, positive numbers.

net

A flat pattern that can be cut out, folded and glued together to make a three-dimensional model of a solid.

Examples:

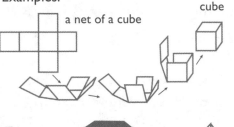

a net of a cube

cube

net of a pyramid

pyramid

See cube, model, pattern, pyramid, table of nets.

network

A system of lines or arcs and intersections (nodes) drawn to represent paths and their intersections.

Examples:

The properties of networks are studied as part of topology.

See intersection, node, topology.

node

A point where straight lines or curves intersect. It is also called a junction.

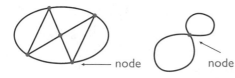

node ←

node

See *intersect, network.*

nonagon

A polygon with nine sides and nine angles.

Examples:

regular nonagon

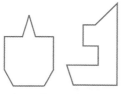

irregular nonagons

See *polygon.*

none

Nothing. Not one. Not any.

Example:

I have two apples

I have none

See *zero.*

non-planar figure

A three-dimensional figure. A solid or space figure.

Examples:

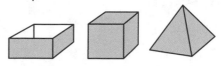

box   cube   square pyramid

Non-planar means 'not in one plane'.

See *planar figure.*

nonstandard unit

Something to help us measure.

Examples:

Handspan, pace, counters, tiles, cubes, squares, and bottle tops are some types of nonstandard units.

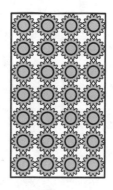

The area of this rectangle has been measured in bottle tops. The area is twenty-eight bottle tops.

See *handspan.*

not equal

(Symbol: ≠)

$$4 \neq 5$$

Four is not equal to five.

See *inequality.*

nothing

(Symbol: 0)

Not one. Having not a thing. Not anything. None.

number

How many things. A measure of quantity.
Numbers are grouped into many different sets:

(i)   Natural (counting) numbers:
      1, 2, 3, 4, 5, 6, …

(ii) Whole numbers:
      0, 1, 2, 3, 4, 5, …

(iii) Integers:
      … ⁻4, ⁻3, ⁻2, ⁻1, 0, ⁺1, ⁺2, ⁺3, …

(iv) Rational numbers, which include fractions:
      $1 : 3$ $\frac{1}{100}$

Other kinds of numbers include complex, composite, prime, odd, even, square, triangular, rectangular, etc.

See composite number, even number, irrational numbers, integer, natural number, odd number, prime number, rational number, rectangular number, square number, triangular number, whole number.

number expander

A folded strip of paper used to learn place value.

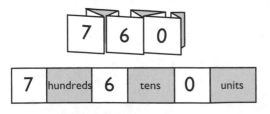

number line

A line on which equally spaced points are marked. The points correspond, in order, to the numbers shown.

Example:

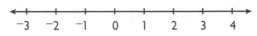

On a number line, the points are labeled from zero. The numbers show the distance from zero to each point (using the distance between successive points as one unit).

Operations with numbers can be shown on a number line.

Example:
Add three and four.

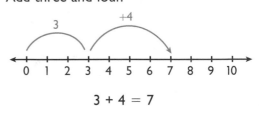

$$3 + 4 = 7$$

See *operations, order.*

number machine

Number machines can carry out operations such as addition, subtraction, multiplication, and division. Calculators and computers are types of number machines.

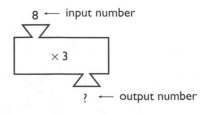

(1) The number 8 is put into the machine. This is the **input** number.
(2) The number is multiplied by three. This is the **rule**.
(3) What comes out is the answer.

See *calculator, rule.*

number pattern

See *pattern.*

number sentence

A statement about numbers, usually in symbols rather than words.

Examples:

6 + 7 = 13	(true)
4 ≠ 9	(true)
5 + □ = 9	(open)
7 + 9 = 10	(false)
3 + 1 < 3 × 1	(false)

See *open number sentence.*

number track

A track, as used in dice games, where the cells are numbered.

Example:

14	13	12	11	10	9	8	7	6	5	4
15	30	29	28	FORWARD TO 35	27	26	25	24	3
16	31	42	41	40	39	38	37	36	23	2
17	GO BACK TO 29	43	GO BACK TO 34	FINISH	35	GO BACK TO 29	1
GO BACK TO 9	GO BACK TO 29	32	GO BACK TO 23	33	34	FORWARD TO 41	GO BACK TO 29	START
18	19	FORWARD TO 30	20	GO BACK TO 13	21	22

numeral

A symbol used to name a number.

Example:

5 is the numeral that names the number five.

5 apples

5 and V (Roman) are numerals for the number five.

See *numeration, Roman numerals, symbol.*

numeration

A system of symbols used to represent numbers. Our system uses the symbols:
0, 1, 2, 3, 4, 5, 6, 7, 8 and 9.

See *Hindu–Arabic, symbol.*

numerator

The top number in a fraction. It describes a number of parts out of the total number of parts.

Example:

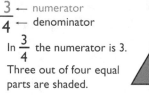

$\dfrac{3}{4}$ ← numerator
← denominator

In $\dfrac{3}{4}$ the numerator is 3.

Three out of four equal parts are shaded.

See *denominator, fraction.*

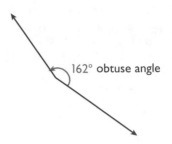

162° obtuse angle

See *angle, right angle, straight angle.*

oblique

A slanting line that is neither vertical nor horizontal.

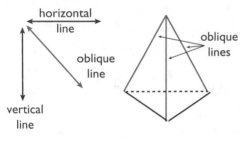

horizontal line

oblique lines

oblique line

vertical line

See *askew.*

oblong

Another word for a rectangle or for rectangular.

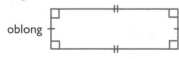

oblong

See *rectangle.*

obtuse angle

An angle bigger than a right angle (90°) but smaller than a straight angle (180°).

Examples:

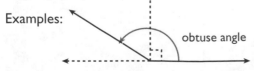

obtuse angle

obtuse triangle

A triangle with one obtuse (larger than 90°) angle.

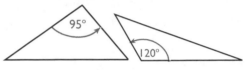

95°

120°

See *acute triangle.*

o'clock

Used when telling time.

Example:
We say: six o'clock, ten o'clock ... only when talking about full hours.

Not used when telling hours and minutes: six fifteen, quarter to seven.

octagon

A plane shape (polygon) with eight sides and eight angles.

Examples:

regular octagon

irregular octagons

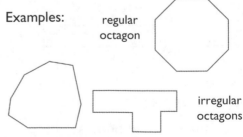

See *plane shape, polygon.*

octahedron

A solid (polyhedron) with eight faces.
A regular octahedron is formed by eight congruent equilateral triangles.

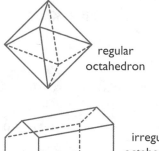

regular octahedron

irregular octahedron

See *polyhedron, regular polyhedron.*

odd number

A number that, when divided by two, leaves a remainder of 1.
All odd numbers end with one of the digits 1, 3, 5, 7 or 9.

See *even number.*

one-dimensional
(1D)

A figure which has only length is said to be one-dimensional.

Examples:
A line has only length; therefore, it has only one dimension.

1D figures

See *dimension, plane.*

one-to-one correspondence

A matching of the objects of two sets.

Examples:
Cups and saucers.
Straws and bottles.
Jumpers and children.

A correspondence between two sets for which each member of each set is paired with only one member of the other set. Arrows are used to show the corresponding objects.

SET A = (Jenny, Dad, Jim)

SET B = (fish, pipe, fishing rod)

See *arrow diagram, correspondence, many-to-one correspondence.*

open curve

A curve that has a beginning and an end which do not meet.

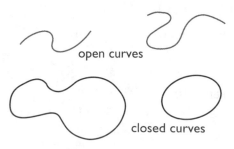

open curves

closed curves

See *closed curve, curve.*

open number sentence

A mathematical sentence that contains numbers and variables. It can be an equation or an inequation.

Examples:

Equations	Inequations
$5 + \triangle = 10$	$4a \neq 9$
$3 \square - 1 = 25$	$5x - 5 < 33$
$\frac{x}{2} - 5 = 7$	$10 - y \geq 28$

See *equation, inequality, inequation, number sentence.*

operation

There are four arithmetic operations:

		Examples:
Addition	$+$	$2 + 4$
Subtraction	$-$	$7 - 3$
Multiplication	$\times$	10×5
Division	$\div$	$8 \div 4$

See *addition, arithmetic, basic facts, division, multiplication, order of operations, subtraction.*

operators

The signs used in operations.

$$+ \quad - \quad \times \quad \div$$

Examples:

$10 + 2 \quad 7 \times 3 \quad 8 - 4 \quad 18 \div 6$

See *operation.*

opposite numbers

Numbers that add up to zero.

Example:

$$-5 + 5 = 0$$

The opposite of -5 is 5; the opposite of 320 is -320.

order

(i) To order means to arrange in a pattern or a sequence.

(ii) Order means a pattern or a sequence.

(iii) Order of numbers on a number line.

See *ascending, descending, number line, pattern, sequence.*

ordered pair

Two numbers (called x-coordinate and y-coordinate) written in a certain order.
Ordered pairs are written with parentheses.

Example: $(5, 3)$

The x-coordinate is always written first. The ordered pair ■ $(3, 5)$ is not the same as the ordered pair ● $(5, 3)$. The point marked 0 is the origin.

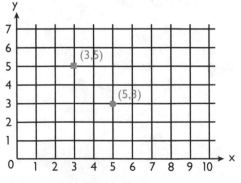

See *axis, brackets, coordinates, origin.*

ordering

Placement according to size, color, numerical value, etc.

Example:

order of operations

Rules for evaluating mathematical expressions.

(i) Number sentences with grouping symbols.

When grouping symbols are used, working is done from inside the brackets out.

Example:

$5 \{3 - [(4 \times 9) - (20 - 4)] + 19\}$

$= 5 \{3 - [36 - 16] + 19\}$

$= 5 \{3 - 20 + 19\}$

$= 5 \times 2$

$= 10$

(ii) When no grouping symbols are used, starting from the left do all multiplications and divisions, then again from the left, do all additions and subtractions.

Example:

$48 \div 3 + 2 - 4 \times 3$

$(48 \div 3) + 2 - (4 \times 3)$ Insert brackets around multiplication and division.

$= 16 + 2 - 12$ Do addition first,
$= 18 - 12$ then subtraction.

$= 6$

(iii) Sometimes "of" is used.

Example:

$5 (3 + 8) - \frac{1}{2}$ of 10

$= 5 \times 11 - (\frac{1}{2} \times 10)$

$= 55 - 5$

$= 50$

Note: To remember the order of operations, do:
Brackets first, Of, Division, Multiplication, Addition, Subtraction.
Think: BODMAS.

See *brackets, grouping symbols, operations.*

ordinal number

A number which indicates position.

Examples: 1st   2nd   3rd   4th

See *cardinal number.*

origin

A point at which something begins.

Example: axis y

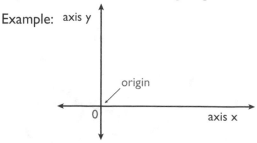

The coordinates of the origin are $(0, 0)$.

The point where axes x and y intersect is called the origin and is marked 0.

See *axis, coordinates, intersect, ordered pair.*

outcome

Result.

Example:

In tossing a coin, there are two possible outcomes, either heads or tails.

output

See *number machine*.

oval

(i) An egg-shaped figure that is symmetrical about one axis. One end is more pointed than the other.

Example:

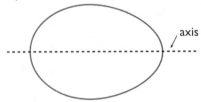

(ii) Another word for an ellipse, which is symmetrical about two axes.

Example:

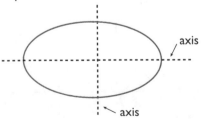

See *axis, ellipse, symmetry*.

p.a.

Per annum. Per year.

Example:
The bank charges 7% interest p.a.

pace

The distance between your feet when you take a step. It is measured from heel to heel. It is used as an arbitrary unit for estimating distances.

— My pace measures 25 inches.

1 pace

See *arbitrary unit, distance, estimate.*

pair

Two things that belong together.

Example:

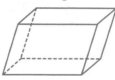

a pair of socks

palindrome

A number or word that reads the same forward as backward.

Examples:
1991   1,991,991   madam

pantograph

An instrument for tracing a drawing, map or a picture. Also used for the enlargement or reduction of an original.

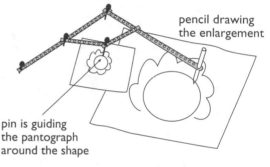

pencil drawing the enlargement

pin is guiding the pantograph around the shape

See *enlargement.*

parallelepiped

A prism, made of parallelograms.

See *parallelogram, prism.*

parallel lines
(Symbols:)

(i)   Two or more lines that go in exactly the same direction. Parallel lines always remain the same distance apart. They never meet.

Examples:

train tracks are parallel

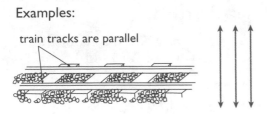

(ii) When parallel lines are crossed by a transversal, pairs of angles are formed. They have special properties:

1 corresponding angles (make F-shape). They are equal.

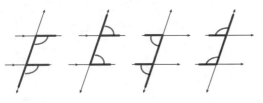

2 alternate angles (make Z-shape). They are equal.

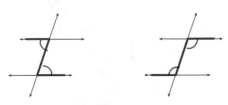

3 cointerior angles (make U-shape). They add up to 180°.

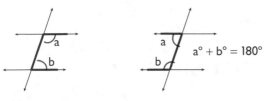

$a° + b° = 180°$

See *transversal, vertically opposite.*

parallelogram

A four-sided figure (quadrilateral) in which both pairs of opposite sides are parallel and equal, and the opposite angles are equal.

Examples:

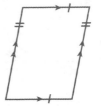

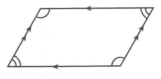

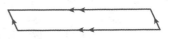

The arrow marks  show which pairs of lines are parallel. A right-angled parallelogram is a rectangle.

Example:

See *parallel lines, quadrilateral, rectangle.*

parentheses

See *brackets.*

partition

See *division.*

Pascal's triangle

A number pattern named for Blaise Pascal, who was a French mathematician from the 17th century.

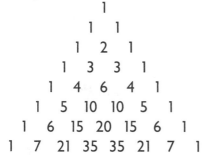

Notice that after the second line the new numbers are made by adding two numbers in the line above and writing a 1 at the beginning and end of the row.

path

A connected set of points. The route or line along which a person or object moves.

Example:

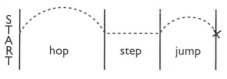

The path of my hop-step-jump

pattern

A repeated design or arrangement using shapes, lines, colors, numbers, etc.

Examples:

(i) Shape pattern

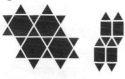

(ii) Color pattern

(iii) A number pattern is a sequence of numbers formed by following a rule.

Examples:

1, 4, 7, 10 ... (rule: add three)

$16, 8, 4, 2, 1, \frac{1}{2}, \frac{1}{4}, \frac{1}{8}$ ...
(rule: divide by two)

See *rule, sequence.*

pattern blocks

Sets of plastic, wood or cardboard shapes in the form of triangles, squares, parallelograms, hexagons, etc.

Examples:

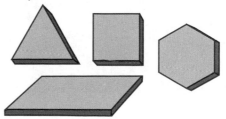

pegboard

Plastic or wooden board containing holes in which pegs can be placed.

Example:

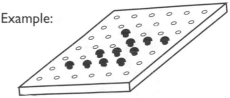

Colored pegs are used to represent numbers, patterns or shapes.

pendulum

A small heavy object attached to a string suspended from a fixed point.

Example:

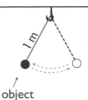

object

If the string is one meter in length, then it takes about one second to make a single complete swing, over and back.

See *second*.

pentagon

A shape (polygon) with five straight sides and five angles.

Examples:

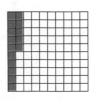

irregular pentagon   regular pentagon

See *polygon*.

percent

(Symbol: %)

A number out of one hundred.

Example:

This is a "hundred square." Fifteen out of the hundred little squares have been shaded in. They represent:

$$\frac{15}{100} = 15\% = 0.15$$

fraction   percent   decimal fraction

See *decimal fraction, fraction*.

perimeter

The distance around a closed shape, or the length of its boundary.

Example:

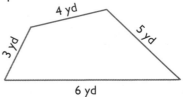

4 yd

3 yd

5 yd

6 yd

To find the perimeter of a shape, add the lengths of all its sides.
The perimeter is:

3 yd + 4 yd + 5 yd + 6 yd = 18 yd

See *boundary, circumference*.

permutation

An ordered arrangement or sequence of a group of objects.

Example:
Three shapes ○ △ □ can be arranged in six different ways, or have six permutations.

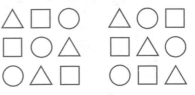

The order in which the shapes are arranged is important in a permutation. When the order is not important, the arrangement is called a combination.

See *combination.*

perpendicular

Forming a right angle.

(i) Perpendicular height

The line segment drawn from the vertex (top) of a figure to the opposite side at a 90° angle.

Examples:

The height of a triangle, cone or pyramid

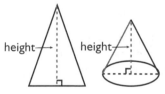

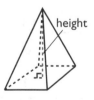

(ii) Perpendicular lines

Lines which intersect to make right angles.

Examples:

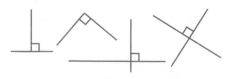

See *altitude, apex, cone, line segment, pyramid, triangle, vertex.*

perspective

When drawing on paper, we can show depth by drawing all parallel lines running into one or several points on the horizon. These points are called vanishing points. The drawing looks like it is three-dimensional. We say it has perspective.

See *converging lines.*

pi
(Symbol: π)

The ratio of the circumference of a circle to its diameter.

$$\pi = \frac{\text{circumference}}{\text{diameter}}$$

The approximate value of π is 3.14. The exact value cannot be worked out.

See *chronological order, circle, circumference, diameter, radius.*

pictograph
(pictogram)

A graph drawn with pictures that represent the real objects.

GRADE 7B - FAVORITE FRUIT

Key: 1 picture stands for 1 person who prefers that fruit

A pictograph must have a title and a key.

See *graph*.

picture graph

Another name for pictograph.

pie chart

A circle graph.

Example:

How Linda spends a day.

See *graph*.

placeholder

(i)   A symbol which holds the place for an unknown number.

Examples:

In w + 3 = 7, w is the placeholder.
In □ − 6 = 10, □ is the placeholder.

(ii) Zero, when used with other digits, is used as a placeholder.

Example: 6,800

The zero in place of ones and tens helps us to see that the digit 8 means eight hundreds, the digit 6 means six thousand and that there are no ones and no tens.

See *digit, equation, variable*.

place value

The value of each digit in a number depends on its place or position in that number.

Examples:

hundreds	tens	units
4	8	6
	1	8
8	2	3

In the number 486 the value of digit 8 is 80 (eight tens).

In the number 18 the value of digit 8 is 8 (eight ones).

In the number 823 the value of digit 8 is 800 (eight hundreds).

See *decimal place-value system, digit, value*.

plan

(i) To prepare ahead of time.

Example: Plan for a holiday.

(ii) A diagram of an object as seen from above.

Example:

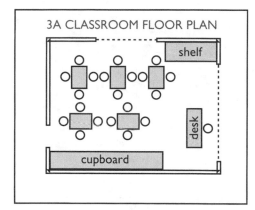

A floor plan of a classroom

See *cross-section, diagram, front view, side view.*

planar figure

A two-dimensional shape, such as a triangle. Also called a plane figure or plane shape.

Examples:

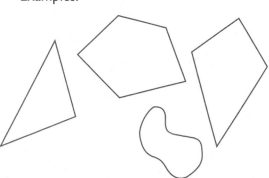

See *plane shape, triangle, two-dimensional.*

plane

A flat surface, like the floor of a house or a wall.

A plane extends infinitely in all directions.

Two-dimensional objects are called plane shapes or planar figures because they can be drawn in one plane.

Example:

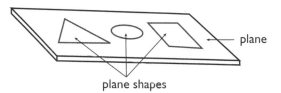

See *dimension, infinite, planar figure, two-dimensional.*

plane shape

A plane shape is a closed shape that lies entirely in one plane.

Examples:

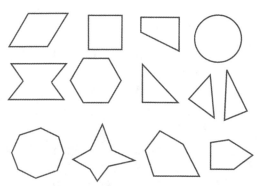

See *non-planar figure, planar figure.*

platonic solids

See *regular polyhedron.*

plus

(Symbol: +)

The name of the symbol that means addition.

Example:

$$4 + 6 = 10$$

See *addition.*

p.m.

(post meridiem)

The time from immediately after 12 noon until immediately before midnight.

Example:

It is evening.
The time is half
past seven.
It is 7:30 p.m.

See *a.m.*

point

(i) Small dot on a surface. It has no dimension.

. P

The dot shows where the point P is.

(ii) The dot, called the decimal point, shows that 4 means four dollars and 50 is fifty cents.

$4 50

See *decimal point.*

polygon

A plane shape which has three or more straight sides; for example, a triangle, quadrilateral, pentagon or hexagon.

Examples:

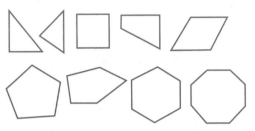

See *closed shape, hexagon, irregular polygon, line segment, octagon, pentagon, quadrilateral, regular polygon, triangle.*

polyhedron

(Plural: polyhedrons or polyhedra)

A three-dimensional shape with plane faces.

Examples:

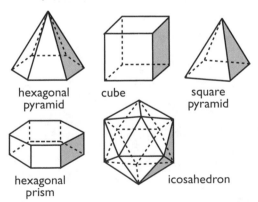

hexagonal   cube   square
pyramid   pyramid

hexagonal   icosahedron
prism

See *cube, dodecahedron, icosahedron, prism, pyramid, regular polyhedron.*

polyomino

A plane shape made of squares of the same size, each square being connected to at least one of the others by a common edge.

Examples:

domino – two squares

triomino – three squares

tetromino – four squares

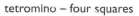

pentomino – five squares

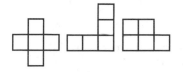

See *planar figure*.

position

Describes the place where something is.

Examples:

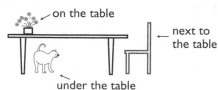

on the table

next to the table

under the table

On, under, above, behind, in front of, between, next to, outside, etc.

See *coordinates, ordered pairs*.

positive numbers

Numbers greater than zero.

Examples:

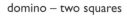

$$-6 \;\; -5 \;\; -4 \;\; -3 \;\; -2 \;\; -1 \;\; 0 \;\; +1 \;\; +2 \;\; +3 \;\; +4 \;\; +5 \;\; +6$$

$+4, +5, +6 \ldots +937, +938 \ldots$

See *integers, negative numbers*.

power of a number

In 2^4 the power is 4.
It means $2 \times 2 \times 2 \times 2 = 16$.
Say: *two to the fourth power*.
When the power is zero, the value is one.

$10^0 = 1$ $1,000^0 = 1$

See *cubed number, square of a number, zero power*.

prediction

In mathematics we can predict or estimate possible answers.

See *estimate, probability*.

prefix

A word before a unit, showing us how large the measure is.

Example:

One millimeter means one thousandth of a meter.

See *Prefixes tables on pages 151–152*.

prime factor of a number

A prime number that will divide exactly into a given number.

Example:

2, 3 and 5 are the prime factors of thirty. (10 is a factor of thirty, but not a prime factor.)

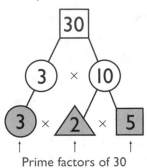

Prime factors of 30

See *factor tree, factors, prime number.*

prime number

A number with exactly two factors, 1 and itself.

Examples:

2, 3, 5, 7, 11, 13, 17 …
The factors of 2 are 2 and 1.
The factors of 5 are 5 and 1.

Note: 1 is considered to be neither prime nor composite.

See *composite number, factor.*

prism

A solid figure with two faces that are parallel and the same in size and shape. They can be any polygon.

Examples:

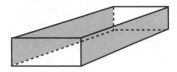

rectangular prism

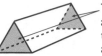

These two faces are parallel and the same shape and size.

triangular prism

All cuboids are prisms.

See *cuboid, face, parallel, polygon, polyhedron, prism, three-dimensional.*

probability

The likelihood of an event happening.

Example:

If a coin is tossed, the probability of getting tails is $\frac{1}{2}$.

See *chance event, equally likely.*

problem solving

Using your understanding and knowledge of mathematical concepts and principles to find a solution in a new or unfamiliar situation.

product

The answer to a multiplication problem.

Example:

$$3 \times 2 = 6$$

multiplicand multiplier product

6 is the product.

See associative property of multiplication, commutative property of multiplication, multiplicand, multiplication, multiplier.

progression

A sequence of numbers following a given rule. The numbers in a progression increase or decrease in a constant way.

(i) If the rule is "add a number." it is called an **arithmetic progression**.

Examples:
Rule: add 3   1, 4, 7, 10, 13, 16, ...
Rule: subtract 2   21, 19, 17, 15, 13, 11, ...

(ii) If the rule is "multiply by a number," it is called a **geometric progression**.

Examples:
Rule: multiply by 4   1, 4, 16, 64, 256, ...
Rule: divide by 2   12, 6, 3, 1.5, 0.75, ...

See decrease, increase, sequence.

projection

The transformation of one shape or picture to another.

Example:

Projecting a picture on a screen

See transformation.

proper fraction

A fraction in which the numerator is less than the denominator.

Examples:

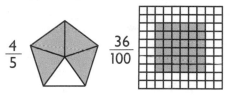

$\frac{4}{5}$ $\frac{36}{100}$

See denominator, fraction, improper fraction, numerator, simple fraction.

property

A characteristic of an object.

See attribute, classification, classify.

proportion

A statement of equality between two ratios.

1 Direct proportion

When a relation between two variables remains constant, they are said to be in direct proportion.

Example:

Mary reads three pages of a book every ten minutes.

The ratio $\frac{pages}{time}$ is constant.

$$\frac{3 \text{ pages}}{10 \text{ min}} = \frac{6 \text{ pages}}{20 \text{ min}} = \frac{9 \text{ pages}}{30 \text{ min}} = \frac{12 \text{ pages}}{40 \text{ min}} \ldots$$

2   Indirect (or inverse) proportion

When one variable is multiplied by a number and the other variable is divided by the same number, they are said to be in indirect proportion.

Example:

It takes four hours for one person to mow the lawn.

It takes two hours for two people to mow the lawn.

Number of people	1	2	3	4	8
Time in hours	4	2	$1\frac{1}{3}$	1	$\frac{1}{2}$

See *inverse proportion, ratio, variable.*

protractor

An instrument used to measure and draw angles.

pyramid

A solid (3D shape) which has a polygon for a base and triangles for all the other faces.

Example:

This pyramid has a square base and the other faces are congruent triangles.

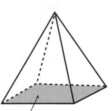

base

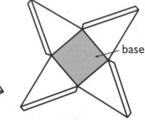

base

A net of a pyramid

A tetrahedron is a pyramid with a triangular base.

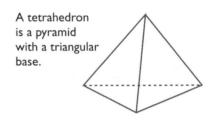

The base of a pyramid can be any polygon.

See *apex, base, face, isosceles triangle, net, polygon, solid, tetrahedron, vertex.*

Pythagorean theorem

In any right triangle, the square of the hypotenuse is equal to the sum of the squares of the sides.

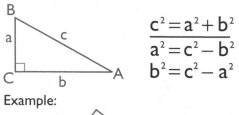

$$c^2 = a^2 + b^2$$
$$a^2 = c^2 - b^2$$
$$b^2 = c^2 - a^2$$

Example:

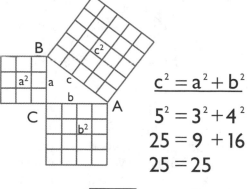

$$c^2 = a^2 + b^2$$
$$5^2 = 3^2 + 4^2$$
$$25 = 9 + 16$$
$$25 = 25$$

$$a = \sqrt{c^2 - b^2}$$
$$b = \sqrt{c^2 - a^2}$$
$$c = \sqrt{a^2 + b^2}$$

quadrilateral

A plane shape with four sides and four angles.

Example:

Some special quadrilaterals are:

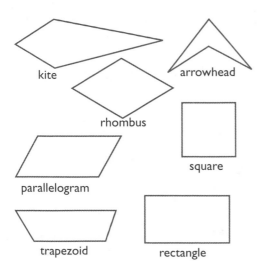

See *kite, parallelogram, planar figure, rectangle, rhombus, square, trapezium.*

quadrant

(i) A quarter of the circumference of a circle.

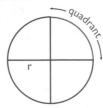

(ii) A plane figure made by two radii of a circle at a 90° angle and the arc cut off by them.

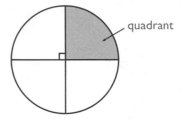

(iii) In coordinate geometry we use the space between the axis-x and axis-y. We can extend the x-axis and the y-axis so that all four quadrants of the number plane can be seen. Quadrants are numbered in a counterclockwise direction.

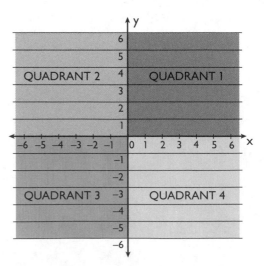

See *arc, coordinates, ordered pair, radius.*

quadruple

Increase the amount four times.

Example:

quadruple $20 means
4 x $20 = $80

See *double, triple.*

quantity

The amount or number
of something.

Example:

The quantity of lemonade in a
bottle is one liter.

quarter

One of four equal parts.

Examples:

$\frac{1}{4}$ is shaded

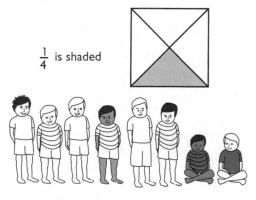

One quarter of the boys are sitting.

quotient

The answer to a division problem.

Example:

$$10 \div 2 = 5$$

dividend   divisor   quotient

Five is the quotient.

See *dividend, division, divisor.*

radian

The radian is the angle at the center of a circle (approximately 57.3°), when the length of the arc is equal to the radius.

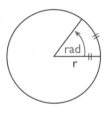

See *arc, radius.*

radiant point

A point from which rays or radii start.

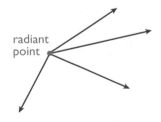

See *ray.*

radius

(Plural: radii)

(i) The distance from the center of a circle to its circumference (or from the center to the surface of a sphere).

Example:

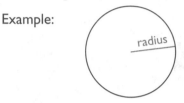

(ii) The line segment joining the center and a point of the circle (like the spoke of a wheel) or a line segment joining the center of a sphere to a point on its surface.

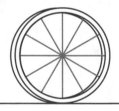

See *circle, circumference, diameter, line segment, sphere.*

random sample

A term in statistics meaning a part or portion which is chosen to represent the whole.

Example:

A bag with twenty black and twenty white balls. A random sample may be three white and two black balls.

See *statistics.*

rate

(i) The comparison between two quantities, which may be of different things.

Example:

Sixty miles per hour (60 mph) is the rate of travel.

ratio

(Symbol:)

A comparison of two quantities. We express one quantity as a fraction of the other.

Example:

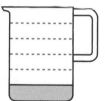

5 parts water

1 part juice

To make a pitcher of juice, mix the juice and water in the ratio of 1 : 5. This means that you mix one part juice to five parts water.

The order of the numbers is important: 1 : 5 ≠ 5 : 1.

See *comparison*.

rational number

A number that can be expressed as a fraction or ratio of integers.

Examples:

$\frac{3}{4}$ $0.5 = \frac{1}{2}$ $8 = \frac{8}{1}$

All rational numbers can be represented by either:

1   Decimal numbers that terminate.

Examples:

$\frac{3}{4} = 0.75$ $\frac{1}{8} = 0.125$

2   Non-terminating, repeating decimals.

Examples:

$\frac{2}{3} = 0.6\bar{6}$ $\frac{-4}{11} = -0.\overline{36}$

See *fraction, ratio, repeating decimal*.

ray

A part of a line. It has a starting point but no endpoint. It extends in one direction only.

Examples:

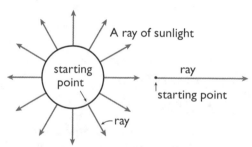

A ray of sunlight

starting point

ray

starting point

ray

See *angle, line, line segment, radiant point*.

reciprocal

The reciprocal of a fraction is the fraction obtained by interchanging the numerator and denominator.

Example:

Reciprocal? Turn the fraction upside down.

(i) Since we can write 4 as $\frac{4}{1}$, the reciprocal of 4 is $\frac{1}{4}$.

(ii) Reciprocal of $\frac{2}{3}$ is $\frac{3}{2}$.

rectangle

A quadrilateral with two pairs of equal and parallel sides, and four right angles.

Example:

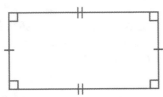

See *parallel, quadrilateral, right angle.*

rectangular numbers

Numbers that can be represented by dots arranged in a rectangle.

Examples:

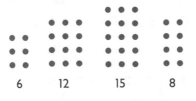

6   12   15   8

rectangular prism

A polyhedron whose base is a rectangle. Another name for a cuboid.

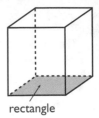
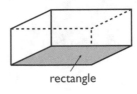

rectangle

rectangle

Most boxes are rectangular prisms.
See *cuboid.*

reduce

(i) Simplify. Express a fraction in its simplest form.

Example:

$\frac{5}{30}$ can be reduced to $\frac{1}{6}$

(ii) Make smaller.

See *canceling, enlargement, fraction, transformation.*

reflection

Being reflected. Reflecting.

Examples:

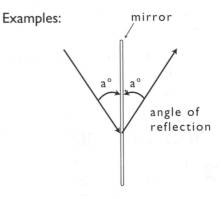

mirror

a°   a°

angle of reflection

See *flip, mirror image.*

reflex angle

An angle greater than a straight angle (180°) but less than a revolution (360°).

Examples:

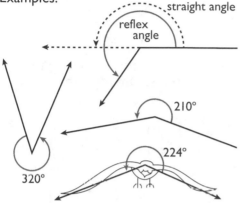

See *angle, revolution, straight angle*.

region

(i) Plane region.

All the points inside a simple closed shape together with all of the points on the boundary of the shape.

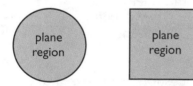

(ii) Solid region.

All the points inside a closed surface together with all the points on the surface.

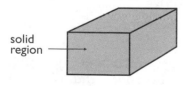

See *boundary, plane, solid, surface*.

regroup

Exchange.

Examples:

(i) Twelve ones blocks can be regrouped (exchanged) for one ten and two ones.

(ii) Before subtracting fifteen, the eight tens and two ones have been regrouped into seven tens and twelve ones.

$$\begin{array}{r} {\scriptstyle 7\ 12} \\ \not{8}\not{2} \\ -15 \\ \hline 67 \end{array}$$

See *carrying, group, base ten blocks*.

regular polygon

A polygon is regular if its sides are equal in length and its angles are equal in size.
Some common regular polygons are:

Equilateral triangle	three sides
Square	four sides
Regular pentagon	five sides
Regular hexagon	six sides

equilateral triangle   square

regular pentagon   regular hexagon

See *equilateral triangle, hexagon, irregular polygon, pentagon*.

regular polyhedron

A polyhedron whose faces are congruent regular polygons, that are exactly the same in shape and size. Internal angles are also the same in size. Regular polyhedrons are also called platonic solids. There are only five regular polyhedrons:

tetrahedron   hexahedron (cube)   dodecahedron

octahedron   icosahedron

See *congruent, dodecahedron, face, hexahedron, icosahedron, octahedron, polyhedron, tetrahedron.*

regular shape

See *regular polygon.*

relation

Connection, correspondence or contrast between a pair of objects, measures, numbers, etc. Also called relationship.

Examples:

(i) Family relationship: Judi is the sister of Lea.

(ii) Size relation: Jan is taller than Helen.

(iii) Mathematical relation.

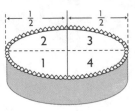

2 is half of 4

(iv) Relation between pairs of numbers. Often presented in a table.

x	1	2	3	4	5
y	6	7	8	9	10

$$y = x + 5$$

See *arrow diagram, correspondence.*

remainder

The amount left over after division.

Example:

There are different ways of expressing the remainder in the answer. They depend on the question.

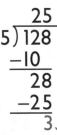

Examples:

(i) Question: Five boys share 128 marbles. How many marbles each?

Answer: Each boy gets 25 marbles. 3 marbles are left over.

(ii) Question: Share $128 among five girls.

Answer: Each girl gets $25 and $\frac{3}{5}$ of a dollar; that is, $25 and 60¢.

See *division.*

rename

Change expression.

Examples:

(i) Rename kilograms as grams.
     $1\frac{3}{4}$ kg = 1750 g = 1.75 kg
(ii) Rename fractions as mixed
     numbers.
     $\frac{7}{3} = 2\frac{1}{3}$

repeating decimal

A decimal fraction in which one or
more digits are repeated
indefinitely.

Examples:

(i) $\frac{1}{3}$ = 0.33333... = $0.\overline{3}$

     It is written $0.\overline{3}$. The bar shows
     that the digit is repeated.

(ii) $0.\overline{17}$

     The bar shows that the digits
     1 and 7 are repeated.

     0.1717171717...

(iii) $\frac{1}{7}$ = 0.142857142857 ...

     It is written as $0.\overline{142857}$ to
     show the repeating digits.

See *decimal fraction, rational number,
terminating decimal.*

reverse

The other way round, or opposite
way round.

Example:

The reverse of 385 is 583.

revolution

One complete turn. There are 360°
in one revolution.
There are four right angles in one
revolution.

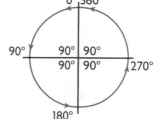

See *angle, right angle.*

rhombus

A shape (parallelogram) with four
equal sides. Opposite angles are
equal.

Examples:

See *diamond, parallelogram.*

right angle

(Symbol: ⌐)

An angle measuring exactly 90°.

Examples:

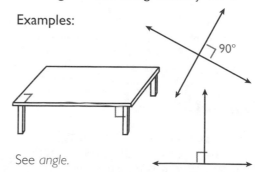

See *angle.*

right triangle

A triangle with a right angle.

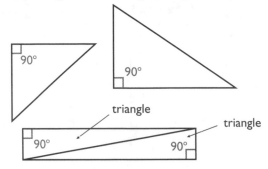

See *Pythagorean theorem, right angle.*

right 3D shape

A solid with ends or base perpendicular to height.

Examples:

right cone

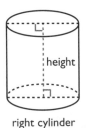

right cylinder

right prism

See *cone, cylinder, prism.*

rigid

Not flexible. Stiff. A jointed structure is rigid when its angles cannot be changed (the sides will not move out of place).

A triangle forms a rigid structure.

 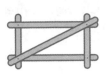

rigid shape   rigid shape

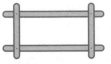

non-rigid shape (flexible)

See *flexible.*

Roman numerals

An ancient system of numeration, where the numbers are represented by letters of the Roman alphabet.

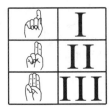 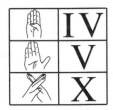

The numerals are made up of a combination of these symbols.

I	(1)	C	(100) centum
V	(5)	D	(500)
X	(10)	M	(1,000) mille
L	(50)		

Examples:
2000 — MM
2002 — MMII

See *numeration, Useful Information page 147.*

rotate

Move around an axis or center.
Revolve. Turn round and round.

Examples:

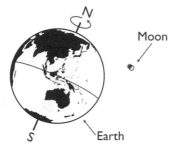

The Earth rotates around its axis.
The Moon revolves around the earth.

rotation

The process by which an object
changes position by turning about
a fixed point through a given
angle.

Examples:

quarter turn　　　　　　half turn
(a rotation through 90°)　(a rotation through 180°)

three-quarter turn
(a rotation through 270°)

rotational symmetry

When a shape is turned through
an angle less than 360° and
remains the same, it has rotational
symmetry.

Example:

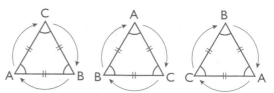

An equilateral triangle has rotational symmetry.

round

To replace a number by the nearest
ten, hundred, thousand, and so on.

Example:

2,764　rounded to the nearest ten
　　　　becomes 2,760

　　　　rounded to the nearest
　　　　hundred becomes 2,800

　　　　rounded to the nearest
　　　　thousand becomes 3,000

Numbers ending in 1, 2, 3, and 4
round down to the lower number.

Examples:

54　　rounded to the nearest ten
　　　becomes 50.

348　rounded to the nearest
　　　hundred becomes 300.

Numbers ending in 5, 6, 7, 8 and 9
round up to the higher number.

Examples:

55　　rounded to the nearest 10
　　　becomes 60.

356   rounded to the nearest
100 becomes 400.

See *accurate, estimate, significant figures.*

....

route

A path. A way taken from start to finish.

Example:

My route to school

....

row

(i)   A horizontal arrangement.

Example:

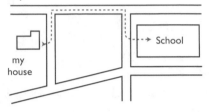

3 rows of pears

(ii) Things arranged so that they make a line going from left to right.

Example:

A row of numbers: 4, 5, 6, 7, 8, 9, ...

See *column, horizontal.*

....

rule

(i)   An instruction to do something in a particular way.

Example:
Find the rule for this sequence.

$$1, 4, 7, 10, 13$$
+3   +3   +3   +3

The rule is "add 3."

(ii) Numbers in a relation are following a rule.

Example:

t	1	2	3	4	5	6
D	15	30	45	60	75	90

The rule is $D = 15t$

(iii) To draw a line using a ruler.

See *number machine, progression, sequence.*

....

ruler

An instrument for drawing straight lines, usually made of plastic or wood. It has a scale for measuring length.

See *graduated, scale.*

scale

(i) A thermometer, a ruler or a balance has a scale marked on it to measure temperature, length and weight.

Examples:

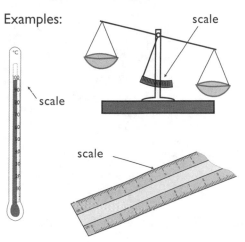

s

Symbol for second.

same

Identical, alike, unchanged, not different.

Example:

See *congruent.*   same shapes

sample

A selection of a few items taken from a larger set.

Example:

In a biscuit factory they take a sample of each batch of biscuits.

satisfy

In mathematics it means "make the equation true."

Example:

If x < 5, which of the numbers 8, 3, 35 or 4 satisfy the inequation?

Answer: 3 and 4, because 3 < 5 and 4 < 5.

(ii) A number line used on a graph.

Example:

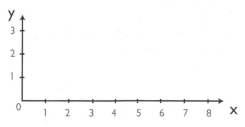

(iii) The scale on a map or a plan shows the ratio for making things larger or smaller.

Example:

SCALE
1 cm = 10 km

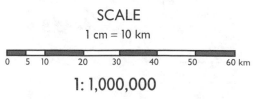

1: 1,000,000

See *balance, enlarge, graph, number line, reduce.*

scale drawing

A drawing or plan on which the real object is made bigger or smaller while keeping the same proportions.

Example:

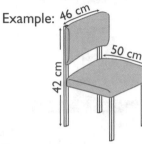

The child's chair was made similar to the adult's chair on a scale 1 to 2 or 1 : 2.

See *proportion*.

scalene triangle

A triangle with each side different in length.

See *right 3D shape, triangle*.

scales

Instruments used for finding or comparing weights or masses.

Examples:

A balance for measuring and comparing masses

Spring balance for measuring weight

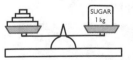

A balance for comparing masses

Bathroom scales

See *mass, weight*.

scientific notation

A shorthand way of writing very large or very small numbers using powers of ten.

Example:

(i) $6,300,000 = 6.3 \times 1,000,000$

$= 6.3 \times 10^6$

6 places

(ii) $0.000567 = 5.67 \times 0.0001$

$= 5.67 \times 10^{-4}$

4 places

See *expanded notation, index notation*.

score

The amount of points or marks gained in a competition or test.

Example:

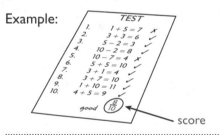

score

second

(i) second (2nd): The ordinal number that comes after first (1st) and before third (3rd).

1st   2nd   3rd

See *ordinal number*.

(ii) second (symbol: s): A measurement of time. There are sixty seconds in one minute.

Example:

One second is the time taken by a pendulum about one meter long to make one complete swing, over and back.

See pendulum

(iii) second in angle measurement (symbol: ")

See degree.

section

(i) A flat surface obtained by cutting through a solid in any direction.

Example:

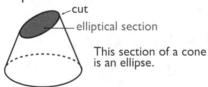

This section of a cone is an ellipse.

(ii) When the cut is parallel to the base of the solid, it is called a cross-section.

Example:

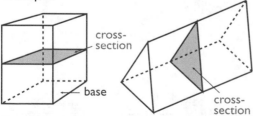

See cone, cross-section, ellipse, flat, frustum, segment, solid, surface.

segment

A part, a section of something.

Examples:
(i) A line segment.

(ii) A segment of a circle is the part of the circle between an arc and its chord.

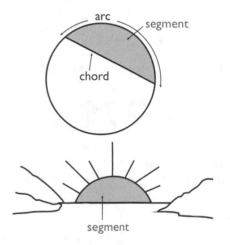

See arc, chord.

semicircle

Half a circle.
When you cut a circle along its diameter, you get two semicircles.

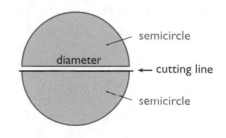

See circle, diameter.

sentence

A statement. In mathematics a sentence may contain variables, numerals, and other symbols.

See *false sentence, number sentence, numeral, open sentence, pronumeral, symbol, true sentence.*

sequence

A pattern, following an order or rule.

Examples:

(i)   1, 3, 5, 7, …

The rule of this sequence is 'add 2'.

(ii)

In this sequence each shape is following a pattern of rotation counterclockwise by quarter turns.

See *counterclockwise, order, pattern, progression, rotation, rule.*

seriate

To put in order.

Example:

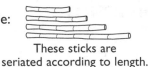

These sticks are seriated according to length.

set

(Symbol: { })

A group of objects or numbers. Each object in a set is called a member or an element of the set. The elements of a set are written inside braces { }.

Example:

Set of whole numbers = $\{0, 1, 2, 3, 4 \ldots\}$

See *braces, cardinal number, element of a set, subset, whole number.*

set square

An instrument used for geometrical drawings, made of wood, plastic or metal.

Examples:

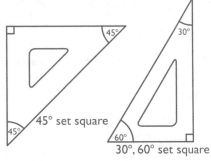

45° set square

30°, 60° set square

Set squares are used for drawing parallel lines, right and other angles, etc.

See *parallel lines, right angle.*

shadow stick measuring

A useful, old method for calculating heights that cannot be directly measured. It is based on the properties of similar triangles.

Example:

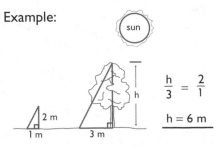

$$\frac{h}{3} = \frac{2}{1}$$

$$h = 6 \text{ m}$$

We measure the shadow of a stick of a known length and the shadow cast by the tall object. The length of the stick and the object, and their shadows, are in the same ratio.

See *ratio, similar.*

shape

The form of an object.

Examples:

2D shapes: triangles, quadrilaterals
3D shapes: cubes, prisms, pyramids

See *cube, dimension, prism, pyramid, quadrilateral, three-dimensional, triangle, two-dimensional.*

sharing

See *division.*

SI

The International metric system. The symbol SI comes from the initials of the French term *Système Internationale d'Unités* (international unit system).

See *metric system.*

side

A line segment that is a part of a perimeter or of a figure.

Example:

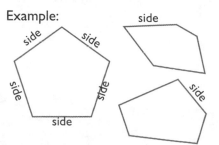

A pentagon has five sides.

See *line segment, pentagon, perimeter.*

side of an angle

One of the rays which make an angle.

Example:

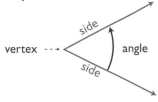

See *angle, vertex.*

side view

A diagram, as seen from the side.

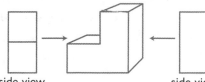

side view　　　　　　　　　side view

See *cross-section, front view, plan.*

sign

A symbol used to show an operation or a statement.

Examples:

Addition sign	+
Subtraction sign	−
Multiplication sign	×
Division signs	÷ ⟍
Equal sign	=

See *operation, symbol and the list of symbols on page 146.*

significant figure

A digit in a number that is considered important when rounding or making an approximation.

Examples:

3,745 rounded to two significant figures is 3,700.

0.165 of a meter rounded to one significant figure is 0.2 of a meter.

See approximate, rounding.

similar

The same in shape but not in size. Two shapes are similar if the corresponding angles are equal and all sides are enlarged or reduced in the same ratio.

Examples:

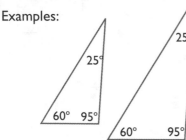

Similar triangles

See congruent, enlarge, ratio, reduce.

simple fraction

A fraction such as $\frac{3}{4}$, $\frac{1}{2}$, $\frac{7}{10}$ in which the numerator is less than the denominator. Also called a proper fraction.

Example:

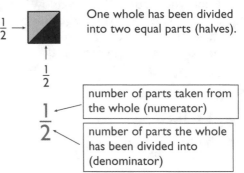

One whole has been divided into two equal parts (halves).

$\frac{1}{2}$

$\frac{1}{2}$ — number of parts taken from the whole (numerator)

$\frac{1}{2}$ — number of parts the whole has been divided into (denominator)

See denominator, fraction, numerator.

simplify

Make simple. Write in the shortest, simplest form.

Example:

Simplify $\dfrac{8}{10} + \dfrac{4}{20}$

$= \dfrac{4}{5} + \dfrac{1}{5}$

$= \dfrac{5}{5}$

$= 1$

Simplify $\dfrac{a^2 b}{ab}$

$= \dfrac{a \times a^1 \times b^1}{a_1 \times b_1}$

$= a$

See canceling.

simultaneous equations

Equations that have the same unknown quantities and are solved together.

Example:

$a + b = 10$
$2a = 6$ ⇒ $\underline{a = 3}$ ✔

$3 + b = 10$
$b = 10 - 3$
$\underline{b = 7}$ ✔

Check:
$a + b = 10$
$3 + 7 = 10$ ✔

The solution is $a = 3$ and $b = 7$.

size

The amount, magnitude, or dimension.

Examples:

(i) The size of this angle is 37°.

(ii) Helen wears size ten clothes and size two shoes.

skew lines

Lines that do not lie in the same plane; they cannot intersect and are not parallel.

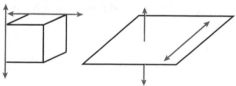

See *intersect, parallel lines.*

slide

Change position on the surface.
See *flip, rotation, translation, turn.*

slope

On a coordinate plane, the steepness of a line. The vertical change is called the "change in y" and the horizontal change is called the "change in x."

$$\text{slope} = \frac{\text{change in y}}{\text{change in x}}$$

solid

A solid is a figure with three dimensions, usually length, width and height (depth).

Examples:

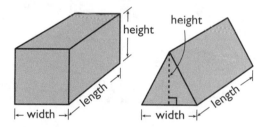

See *height, length, three-dimensional, width.*

solution

The answer to a problem or question.

Example:
The equation $x + 4 = 9$
has a solution $x = 5$.

solve

Find the answer.
See *calculate, solution.*

some

Not all of the whole. At least one.

Examples:

(i)

A whole cake   Some of the cake

(ii) Some of the children are walking away.

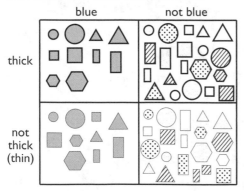

sorting

Putting objects into groups according to attributes.

Example:
Attributes are color and thickness.

See *attribute, Carroll diagram, classification, classify, group.*

space

Space is a three-dimensional region. Spatial figures (solids) have three dimensions.

See *dimension, region, solid, three-dimensional.*

span

Stretch from side to side, across.

See *handspan.*

spatial

Things that are relating to, or happening in, space.

speed

The rate of time at which something travels. The distance travelled in a unit of time.

Example:

A car traveled sixty miles in one hour. Its speed was 60 mph.

See *distance, unit of measurement.*

sphere

A three-dimensional shape like a round ball. A sphere has one curved surface and no corners or edges. Every point on the sphere's surface is the same distance from the sphere's center.

Examples:

A basketball   The earth

See *three-dimensional*.

spinner

A disc marked with numbers used in chance games.

Examples:

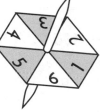

spiral

A curve like a coil on a flat surface.

Example:

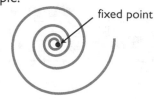

fixed point

A spiral is a continuous curve moving around a fixed point so that its distance from the fixed point is always increasing.

See *curve, distance*.

spring balance

An instrument that measures weight. A spring inside it is extended by the force equal to the weight of the object.

See *weight*.

square

A quadrilateral with four equal sides and four right angles.

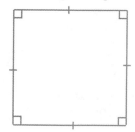

See *quadrilateral, right angle*.

square centimeter

(Symbol: cm²)

A square centimeter is a unit for measuring area.

Examples:

1 cm

1 cm

The area is one square centimeter.

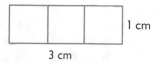

1 cm

3 cm

The area of this shape is three square centimeters.

$$3 \text{ cm} \times 1 \text{ cm} = 3 \text{ cm}^2$$

See *area, unit of measurement*.

square kilometer

(Symbol: km²)

A unit for measuring very large areas.

$$1 \text{ km}^2 = 1,000,000 \text{ m}^2$$

See *area*.

square meter

(Symbol: m²)

A unit for measuring area.

$$1 \text{ m}^2 = 10,000 \text{ cm}^2$$

Examples:

(i) This man is holding a piece of cardboard which has an area of one square meter.

(ii) This rug has an area of 4.5 m².

1.5 m

3 m

See *area*.

square of a number

The result when you multiply a number by itself.

Examples:

$2^2 = 2 \times 2 = 4$

$3^2 = 3 \times 3 = 9$

$(0.5)^2 = 0.5 \times 0.5 = 0.25$

See *exponents, square root*.

square paper

Paper ruled in squares, used for scale drawing and graphing.

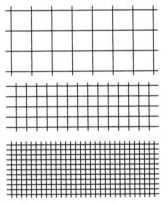

See *scale drawing, graph, isometric paper*.

square number

A number that can be represented by dots in the shape of a square.

Examples:

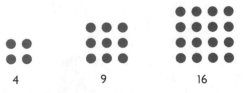

4   9   16

See *rectangular number, triangular number*.

square root

A number that, when multiplied by itself, produces the given number. An inverse operation of squaring a number.

Examples:

$$\sqrt{2} \times \sqrt{2} = 2$$
$$\sqrt{9} \times \sqrt{9} = 9$$
$$\left.\begin{array}{l} {}^{+}2^2 = 2 \times 2 = {}^{+}4 \\ (^{-}2)^2 = {}^{-}2 \times {}^{-}2 = {}^{+}4 \end{array}\right\} \therefore \sqrt{4} = {}^{\pm}2$$

See *square of a number.*

standard

Units of measure that are accepted by agreement are said to be "standard measures."

statistics

The study concerned with the collection and classification of numerical facts. The information collected is called data. Data can be represented in a table or on a graph, and interpreted and analyzed.

Example:

FAVORITE FOODS

Meat	Vegetables	Fruit	Sweets
Paul S.	Carlo	Anne	Dean
John	Hirani	James	Belinda
Tibor		Paul B.	Quong
Jackie		Claire	Brad
Toula		Ranjit	Ali
Sarah			Anna
David			Jhiro
Jeremy			Peter
			Samantha
			Halima

The information in the table is the data. There are 25 children in the class.

8 children prefer meat

$$\therefore \frac{8}{25} \times \frac{100}{1} = 32\%$$ of the class prefer meat.

2 children prefer vegetables

$$\therefore \frac{2}{25} \times \frac{100}{1} = 8\%$$ of the class prefer vegetables.

5 children prefer fruit

$$\therefore \frac{5}{25} \times \frac{100}{1} = 20\%$$ of the class prefer fruit.

10 children prefer sweets

$$\therefore \frac{10}{25} \times \frac{100}{1} = 40\%$$ of the class prefer sweets.

The percentages are statistics about food preferences of the class.

See *data, per cent.*

straight angle

An angle of 180°.

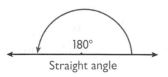

Straight angle

See *angle.*

straightedge

An object that can be used to draw straight lines.

Example:

Chalkboard ruler

straight line

See *line, line segment*.

subset

A set within a set.

Examples:

(i) If each element of a set S (below) is also an element of a set T, then S is called a subset of T.

Set T = {Natural numbers to twenty-five}

Set S = {Square numbers to twenty-five}

(ii) Set A = {all children in your class}

Set B = {all girls in your class}

Set B is a subset of set A, because all the elements in set B are also in set A.

See *combination, set*.

substitution

(i) Something standing in place of another.

(ii) The replacement of a variable (a letter in a code message or a placeholder in a number sentence) by a number.

Examples:

1   If a = 5 and b = 2, what is value of 2a + 2b?

$$2a + 2b = 2 \times 5 + 2 \times 2$$
$$= 10 + 4$$
$$= 14$$

2   In this secret code, numbers are substituted for letters.

A	B	C	D	E	F	G	...		2	1	4	7	5
1	2	3	4	5	6	7	...		B	A	D	G	E

See *code, number sentence, place holder, variable*.

subtract

Take away.
Find the difference.

See *difference, subtraction*.

subtraction

(i) Taking away (finding what is left).

Jessica had five pencils and gave three to Mario. How many pencils did Jessica keep?

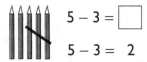

$5 - 3 = \boxed{}$

$5 - 3 = 2$

Jessica kept 2 pencils.

(ii) Difference (comparison).

Remy has seven pencils and Robin has three pencils. How many more pencils has Remy than Robin?

Remy $7 - 3 = \boxed{}$

Robin $7 - 3 = 4$

Remy has 4 more pencils than Robin.

(iii) Complementary addition (missing addend, counting on).

Rowan has three pencils, but needs seven. How many more must he get?

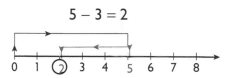

$3 + \boxed{4} = 7$

$3 + \ \ 4 \ = 7$

Rowan must get 4 more pencils.

Subtraction may be represented on a number line:
Show on the number line:

$$5 - 3 = 2$$

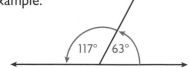

0　1　②　3　4　5　6　7　8

See *complementary addition, difference, number line.*

subtrahend

A number which is to be subtracted from another number.

Example: $12 - 4 = 8$

minuend　　subtrahend　　difference

Four is the subtrahend.

See *difference, minuend, subtract.*

sum

The answer to an addition problem. It is the total amount resulting from the addition of two or more numbers, quantities or magnitudes.

Example: $3 + 4 = 7$

addends　　sum

Seven is the sum.

See *addend, addition.*

supplementary angles

Two angles for which the sum of their measures is 180°.

Example:

117°　63°

Angles 117° and 63° are supplementary.
Angle 117° is called the supplement of 63°.
Angle 63° is called the supplement of 117°.

See *complementary angles, parallel lines.*

surface

(i)　The outside of something.

Example: The surface of the tennis ball is furry.

(ii)　The top level of a liquid.

Example: Leaves float on the surface of a lake.

The surface of an object may be flat or curved.

Example:

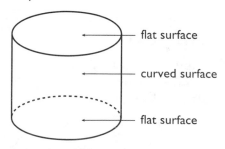

flat surface

curved surface

flat surface

A cylinder has two flat surfaces and one curved.

See *area, cylinder.*

surface area

The total area of the outside of a 3D shape.

Example:

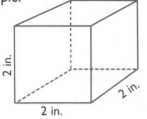

A cube with two-inch sides has a surface area of
$6 \times (2 \times 2)$ in.^{2} = 24 in.^{2}

See area, cube, surface.

symbol

A letter, numeral or mark which represents something.

Examples:

1 2 3 + − × ÷
= ≠ > < ≈ % □
c m   k g   h a   m^3 ∠
a   b   x^2 2x

See abbreviation, place holder, pronumeral, Useful Information page 145.

symmetry

A shape has symmetry or is symmetrical when one half of the shape can fit exactly over the other half.

Shapes are called symmetrical if they have one or more lines (axes) of symmetry.

Examples:

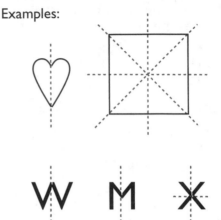

See asymmetry, line of symmetry, rotational symmetry.

Système Internationale d'Unités

See SI.

Example:

The 9s Facts

1 × 9 = 9	6 × 9 = 54
2 × 9 = 18	7 × 9 = 63
3 × 9 = 27	8 × 9 = 72
4 × 9 = 36	9 × 9 = 81
5 × 9 = 45	10 × 9 = 90

See *multiplication.*

t

Symbol for ton.

table

(i) An arrangement of letters or numbers in rows or columns.

Example:

×	1	2	3	4	5	6
1	1	2	3	4	5	6
2	2	4	6	8	10	12
3	3	6	9	12	15	18
4	4	8	12	16	20	24
5	5	10	15	20	25	30
6	6	12	18	24	30	36

(ii) When multiplication facts are arranged in order, they are then called multiplication tables.

take away

Remove, subtract. It is one of the ways of subtraction.

Example:
I had fifteen marbles and I lost seven. How many do I have now?

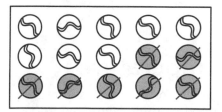

15 − 7 = 8 (take away seven from fifteen)

Answer: I have eight marbles now.
See *subtraction.*

tally marks

A record of items made by placing a mark to represent each item. The marks are usually drawn in groups of five, with the fifth mark in each group crossing the other four, to make them easy to count.

Example: A tally of 13 items

卌 卌 ///

tangram

A Chinese puzzle made up of a square cut into seven pieces that can be rearranged to make many varied shapes.

Example:

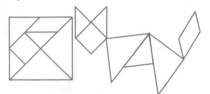

tape measure

A strip of tape or thin metal used to measure length.

temperature

How hot or how cold something is. Temperature is measured in degrees Fahrenheit (°F) or degrees Celsius (°C).

Examples:
(i) Water freezes (changes to ice) at 32°F.

(ii) Water boils at 212°F.
(iii) Normal body temperature is 98.6°F.

See *degree Celsius, thermometer.*

template

An instrument for drawing shapes.

Example:

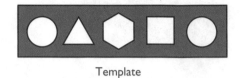

Template

term

(i) Each of two quantities in a ratio or a fraction: $\frac{3}{4}$ 1:7

(ii) Each of the quantities connected by + or − in an algebraic expression or equation.

$3a - 3b$ $y = x + 1$

terminate

To come to an end, finish, not to go any further.

terminating decimal

A decimal fraction that is not repeating, that has "an end."

Example:

$$\frac{1}{4} = 0.25$$

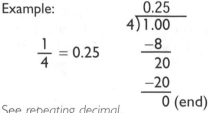

See *repeating decimal.*

tessellation

A complete covering of a plane by one or more figures in a repeating pattern, with no overlapping of, or gaps between, the figures. Mosaic and pavement shapes tessellate.

Examples:

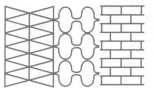

These shapes tessellate.   Circles do not tessellate.

Certain shapes will cover a surface completely: squares, equilateral triangles, hexagons, etc. These are said to "tessellate."

tetrahedron

A solid (polyhedron) with four faces. Also called triangular pyramid.
A regular tetrahedron is made of four congruent equilateral triangles and belongs to the group called platonic solids.

Examples:

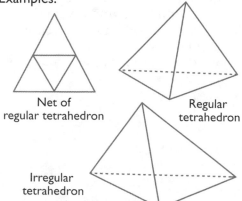

Net of regular tetrahedron

Regular tetrahedron

Irregular tetrahedron

See *polyhedron, regular polyhedron.*

thermometer

An instrument for measuring temperature.

Example:

This thermometer shows a temperature of 100°C.

See *degree Celsius, temperature.*

third

The ordinal number that comes after second and before fourth.

Example:

    1st   2nd   3rd   4th

See *ordinal number.*

thousand

Ten hundreds, written as 1,000.
See *hundred.*

three-dimensional
(3D)

When something has length, width and height, that is, three dimensions, then it is three-dimensional. Space figures (solids) are three-dimensional.

Example:

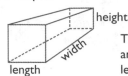

height

The sketch produces an illusion of width, length and height.

length

width

See dimension, solid.

time interval

The time that passes between two events.
Some units of time are:

second	s
minute	min
hour	h
day	d

week, month, year, decade, century, millenium

See unit of measurement.

time line

A line on which intervals of time are recorded in chronological order.

Example:

1990	Dana is born
1993	Will is born
1995	Dana starts kindergarten
1997	Move to new house
1998	Will starts kindergarten
1999	Family vacation in Florida
2001	Dana wins math contest

See time interval.

times
(Symbol: ×)

A word used for multiplication.

Examples:
When we multiply 3×5, we say 'three times five'.

Also, in $5(a + b)$, we say 'five times $(a + b)$'.

ton
(Symbol: t)

A ton is a unit for measuring weight.

$$1 \text{ t} = 2000 \text{ lb}$$

Examples:

The weight of this empty truck is about 1.5 tons.

topology

The part of mathematics that deals with non-measurable properties of things; of insides and outsides, surfaces, shapes and connections. Topology is concerned with relative positions, not measurement.

Example:

Square ABCD can be distorted to look like this:

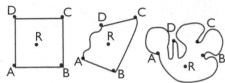

R always remains inside the figure.

Topology is sometimes called "rubber-sheet geometry."

See *property.*

total

(i)   Sum. When you add things or values together, the answer is the total.

Example:

$$10 + 20 + 25 = 55$$

total

(ii) Whole.

Example:

The total area of the farm is 80 hectares.

See *add, sum.*

transformation

(i)   The process by which the shape, position or size of an object is changed.

See *enlarge, flip, projection, reduce, reflection, rotation, translation.*

(ii) The process by which the form of an expression is changed.

Examples: $\frac{1}{2} = 0.5 = 50\%$

The formula for finding the area:
$A = l \times w$, can be transformed into:

$$l = \frac{A}{w}$$

(iii) The process by which a set of numbers (or objects) is associated in one-to-one or many-to-one correspondence with another set of numbers (or objects).

See *many-to-one correspondence, one-to-one correspondence.*

translation

When a shape is moved along a straight line without being flipped, rotated, or reflected, we say it has been translated.

Example:

See *flip, reflection, rotation, slide, turn.*

transversal

A straight line crossing two or more lines.

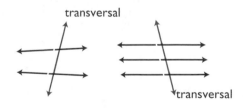

See *line, parallel lines.*

trapezium

A quadrilateral with no parallel sides.

trapezoid

A four-sided figure (quadrilateral) with one pair of sides parallel and the other pair not parallel.

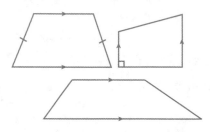

See *isosceles triangle, parallel, quadrilateral.*

traversable

A curve or route is traversable if it can be traced without lifting the pencil or going over any part of the curve more than once.

Examples:

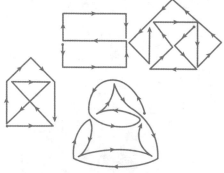

These routes are traversable.

triangle

A polygon with three sides and three angles. We can classify triangles by sides or by angles.

(i) By sides

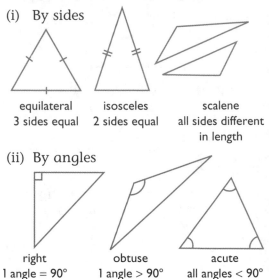

equilateral	isosceles	scalene
3 sides equal	2 sides equal	all sides different in length

(ii) By angles

right	obtuse	acute
1 angle = 90°	1 angle > 90°	all angles < 90°

The sum of angles inside a triangle is always 180°.

See *equilateral triangle, isosceles triangle, plane shape, right triangle, scalene triangle, sum.*

triangle number

(triangular number)

A number that can be represented by dots in the shape of a triangle.

Examples:

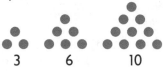

3   6   10

See *triangle.*

trillion

A trillion is a million millions, that is, 1,000,000,000,000, or 10^{12}.

See *Large numbers on page 150.*

triple

Make three times bigger or multiply by three.

See *multiplication.*

true sentence

A sentence about numbers that is true or correct.

Examples:

$3 \times 2 = 2 \times 3$ is a true sentence.

$6 \neq 5$ is a true sentence.

The open sentence $2 + \square = 9$ becomes true, if $\square$ is replaced by 7. If $\square$ is replaced by any other number, then it will become a false sentence.

See *false sentence, number sentence, open sentence.*

trundle wheel

A wheel, usually one meter in circumference, used for measuring distance. The wheel often gives a click sound at each revolution (one meter), so the number of meters can be counted.

See *circumference, meter.*

turn

Move. Change position. Rotate.

See *rotation.*

twelve-hour time

A period of one day (twenty-four hours) divided into two halves of twelve hours each.
Twelve-hour time should include a.m. and p.m.

Example:

This clock shows either 7:45 a.m. or 7:45 p.m.

See *a.m., p.m., twenty-four hour time.*

twenty-four-hour time

A period of one day divided into twenty-four hourly divisions, to prevent errors between a.m. and p.m. times.

Example:

A 24-hour clock

12-hour time	24-hour time
1 a.m.	0100 one hundred hours
10 a.m.	1000 ten hundred hours
1 p.m.	1300 thirteen hundred hours
3:40 p.m.	1540 fifteen-forty hours

See *a.m., p.m., twelve-hour time.*

twice

Two times, or double.

Example:
Twice six is $2 \times 6 = 12$

two-dimensional
(2D)

When something has length and width, then it has two dimensions and is two-dimensional. Plane shapes and surfaces have two dimensions.

Examples:

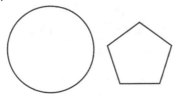

Plane regions have two dimensions.

See *dimension, length, plane shape, region, surface, width.*

$$5 \text{ kg} = \$14.50$$

$$1 \text{ kg} = \frac{\$14.50}{5} = \$2.90$$

$$3 \text{ kg} = \$2.90 \times 3 = \$8.70$$

unit, basic

Units, including those for weight, length and time, form the basis for a system of measurement.

See *unit of measurement.*

unequal

(Symbol: ≠)

Not equal.

Example:

$$3 \neq 4$$

Read as:
'Three is not equal to four'.

See *inequality, not equal.*

union

Combining two or more things.

unit

Unit is another name for one.

unitary method

A simple way of solving problems, by working out the value of one unit.

Example:
Five kilograms of grapes cost $14.50. How much for three kilograms?

unit of measurement

A standard unit such as a mile, pound, minute, quart.

See *standard.*

unit square

A square with sides of length equal to one unit of length or distance.

Example:
A square with sides one meter long has an area of one square meter (1 m^2).

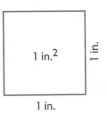

1 in.^{2} 1 in.

1 in.

See *distance, unit of measurement.*

unknown value

In number sentences, algebraic expressions, or equations, the unknown values are represented by variables.

Examples:

$$2\,\square = 10 \qquad x - 7 \geq 5$$

unknown value   unknown value

$$2a - 2b$$

unknown values

See *number sentence, variable*.

unlike terms

Terms that are not like.

Examples:

$$2a + 3b \qquad\qquad 2a + a$$

unlike terms   like terms

Unlike terms cannot be combined or simplified by adding or subtracting.

See *like terms*.

V

Symbol for volume.

value

(i) When an expression is simplified, the result is the value of the expression.

Example: $\frac{3+5}{2} \times 7$

$= \frac{8}{2} \times 7$

$= 4 \times 7$

$= 28$

28 is the value of $\frac{3+5}{2} \times 7$

(ii) When solving equations, we evaluate them.

Example:

Find the value of $\frac{x+5}{2}$, if $x = 10$.

Answer : $\frac{10+5}{2} = 7.5$

7.5 is the value.

(iii) The amount of money something is worth.

Example:

This tape player costs $28.
Its value is $28.

See *equation, evaluate, place value, substitute.*

vanishing point

In perspective, the point or points at which all parallel lines appear to meet.

vanishing point

See *perspective.*

variable

(i) A symbol or letter representing an unknown member of a set. In algebraic expressions, a variable stands for a value. Sometimes it is called an unknown.

Example:
In $x^2 + 3x + 2 = 0$, x is the variable.

(ii) The same variable may have different values under different conditions.

Example:

$x + 3 = 5 \qquad x = 2$

$x - 1 = 10 \qquad x = 11$

(iii) A mathematical sentence that has at least one variable is called an open sentence.

Example:

$x + 3 = 7$ is true only when $x = 4$.

The number 4 is called the solution of $x + 3 = 7$.

If x is replaced by any other number, the sentence will become not true (false).

See *algebra, algebraic expression, number sentence, open sentence, placeholder, symbol.*

Venn diagram

A diagram used to represent sets and relationships between sets.

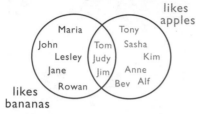

likes apples

likes bananas

See *diagram, set.*

vertex

(Plural: vertices)

Top, the highest part or point. A point where two or more adjacent lines meet to form an angle or a corner.

Example:

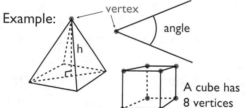

vertex

angle

A cube has 8 vertices

In plane or solid figures, the vertex is the point opposite the base.

See *apex, arm of an angle.*

vertical

A vertical line is perpendicular (at right angles) to the horizon.

Examples:

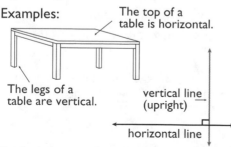

The top of a table is horizontal.

The legs of a table are vertical.

vertical line (upright)

horizontal line

See *axis, horizon, horizontal line, perpendicular, right angle.*

vertically opposite angles

When two lines intersect, they make four angles at the vertex. The angles opposite each other are equal in size and are called vertically opposite angles.

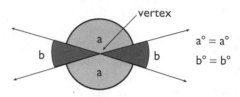

vertex

$a° = a°$

$b° = b°$

See *complementary angles, parallel lines, supplementary angles, vertex.*

volume

The amount of space inside a container, or the actual amount of material in the container.

Example:

The volume of this object is **36 cubic units**.

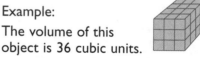

See *capacity, cubic unit, solid.*

Astronaut in space:
His mass is still 75 kg.
But he is weightless.

week

A period of time: seven days. There are fifty-two weeks in a year.

See *days of the week*.

See *mass*.

whole numbers

Zero together with all counting numbers.

$\{0, 1, 2, 3, 4, 5, 6, 7, 8, \ldots\}$

See *counting number, zero*.

weight

The pull of gravity on an object. The true meaning of the term "weight" is a complicated physics problem. The weight of an object changes with the change of the gravitational pull. The mass of an object (the amount of matter the object is made of) remains constant.

Example:

Astronauts become weightless in space but the mass of their bodies does not change.

width

The measurement from side to side.

Example:

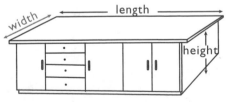

The width of this kitchen bench is 70 in.

Astronaut on Earth:
His mass = 75 kg
His weight ≈ 75 kg

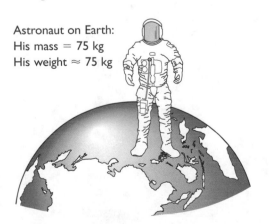

x-axis y-axis

See *coordinates.*

yard

A measure of length.

1 yard = 36 inches

year

The period of time it takes the earth to make one complete revolution around the Sun: 365 days, 5 hours and 48 minutes. The extra hours, minutes and seconds are put together into an extra day every four years to form a leap year.

See *day, leap year, revolution.*

zero

(Symbol:0 ,0)

The numeral 0. Nothing.
Rules for working with zero:
1 A number + 0 = same number

$$5 + 0 = 5$$

2 A number − 0 = same number

$$7 - 0 = 7$$

3 A number $\times$ 0 = 0

$$6 \times 0 = 0$$

4 0 ÷ any number = 0

$$0 \div 10 = 0$$

5 A number ÷ 0 has no answer.

$$3 \div 0 \text{ is not possible.}$$

The digit zero is used as a place holder in numerals.

Example:

In the number sixty, 0 is a place holder for units to show that the 6 means six tens and there are no ones.

Note: These words all mean zero: nil, nought, none, nix, null, void, empty set, zilch.

See *digit, placeholder.*

zero power

When working with exponents, any number raised to the power zero always equals one. It happens because when we divide exponents, we subtract the exponents and get zero.

$$2^0 = 1 \qquad 376^0 = 1 \qquad x^0 = 1$$

Example:
Find the value of:

$$5^2 \div 5^2 \qquad\qquad 5^2 \div 5^2$$

$$= 5 \times 5 \div 5 \times 5 \qquad = 5^{(2-2)}$$

$$= 25 \div 25 \qquad\qquad = 5^0$$

$$= 1 \qquad\qquad\qquad = 1$$

See *exponent, power.*

Useful Information

units of measurement

customary

length

1 foot (ft) = 12 inches (in.)
1 yard (yd) = 3 feet
1 yard = 36 inches
1 mile (m) = 5,280 feet

capacity

1 cup (c) = 8 ounces (oz)
1 pint (pt) = 2 cups
1 pint = 16 ounces
1 quart (qt) = 2 pints
1 gallon (gal) = 4 quarts

weight

1 pound (lb) = 16 ounces
1 ton (t) = 2,000 pounds

time

60 seconds (s)	= 1 minute (min)
60 minutes	= 1 hour (h)
24 hours	= 1 day (d)
7 days	= 1 week
365 days	= 1 year
366 days	= 1 leap year
12 months	= 1 year
10 years	= 1 decade
100 years	= 1 century
1,000 years	= 1 millennium

angle measure

1 degree (1°)	= 60 minutes (60')
1 minute (1')	= 60 seconds (60")
1 right angle	= 90 degrees (90°)
1 straight angle	= 180 degrees (180°)
1 revolution	= 360 degrees (360°)

metric

length

10 millimeters (mm)	= 1 centimeter (cm)
10 centimeters	= 1 decimeter (dm)
100 centimeters	= 1 meter (m)
1,000 meters	= 1 kilometer

capacity

1,000 millileters (mL)	= 1 liter (L)

mass

1,000 milligrams (mg)	= 1 gram (g)
1,000 grams	= 1 kilograms (Kg)
1 tonne	= 1,000 kilograms

abbreviations

in.	inch
ft	foot
yd	yard
mi	mile
oz	ounce
c	cup
pt	pint
qt	quart
gal	gallon
m	meter
g	gram
L	liter
t	ton
m^2	square meter
m^3	cubic meter
ha	hectare
°F	degree Fahrenheit
°C	degree Celsius

a list of symbols

Symbol	Meaning	Example
$+$	addition sign, add, plus	$2 + 1 = 3$
$-$	subtraction sign, subtract, take away, minus	$7 - 6 = 1$
$\times$	multiplication sign, multiply by, times	$3 \times 3 = 9$
$\div$ $)\overline{}$	division sign, divide by	$9 \div 2 = 4.5$
$=$	is equal to, equals	$2 + 2 = 1 + 3$
$\neq$	is not equal to	$2 \neq 5$
$\doteq \approx \cong$	is approximately equal to	$302 \approx 300$
$\leq$	is less than or equal to	$x \leq 12$
$\geq$	is greater than or equal to	$5 \geq y$
$>$	is greater than	$7 > 6.9$
$<$	is less than	$2 < 4$
$\not<$	is not less than	$6 \not< 5$
$\not>$	is not greater than	$3.3 \not> 3.4$
¢	cent(s)	50¢
\$	dollar(s)	\$1.20
.	decimal point	5.24
%	per cent, out of 100	50%
$^\circ$	degree (temperature), degree (angle measure)	70°F $\quad 35^\circ$C $\quad 90^\circ$
$'$	minutes (angle measure)	$5^\circ\,35'$
$'$	foot	$1' = 12$ in.
$''$	seconds (angle measure)	$12^\circ05'24''$
$''$	inch	$12'' = 1'$
$\angle$	angle	$\angle$ AOB
$\triangle$	triangle	$\triangle$ ABC
$\parallel$	parallel lines, is parallel to	AB $\parallel$ CD
╪ ╫	line segments of the same length	
∟	right angle, 90°	
⊥	is perpendicular to, at 90°	$\quad$ h ⊥ b
$\sqrt{}$	square root	$\sqrt{4} = \pm 2$
$\sqrt[3]{}$	cube root	$\sqrt[3]{27} = 3$
π	pi, $\pi \approx 3.14$	$C = 2\pi r$
$\cong$	is congruent to	$\triangle$ ABC $\cong$ $\triangle$ DEF

Roman numerals

	Thousands	Hundreds	Tens	Ones
1	M	C	X	I
2	MM	CC	XX	II
3	MMM	CCC	XXX	III
4		CD	XL	IV
5		D	L	V
6		DC	LX	VI
7		DCC	LXX	VII
8		DCCC	LXXX	VIII
9		CM	XC	IX

EXAMPLE: 1   9   9   9 = MCMXCIX
              ↓   ↓   ↓   ↓
             M CM XC IX

parts of a circle

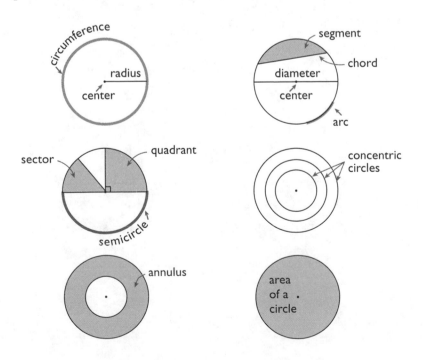

formulas

Plane shapes	Diagram	Area	Perimeter
circle		$A = \pi r^2$	$C = 2\pi r = \pi d$
square		$A = s^2$	$P = 4s$
rectangle		$A = lw$	$P = 2(l + w)$
kite		$A = \dfrac{ab}{2}$	
trapezoid		$A = \dfrac{1}{2} h (b_1 + b_2)$	
parallelogram		$A = bh$	$P = 2(b + h)$
rhombus		$A = sh$	$P = 4s$
triangle		$A = \dfrac{1}{2} bh$	$P = s + s + s$

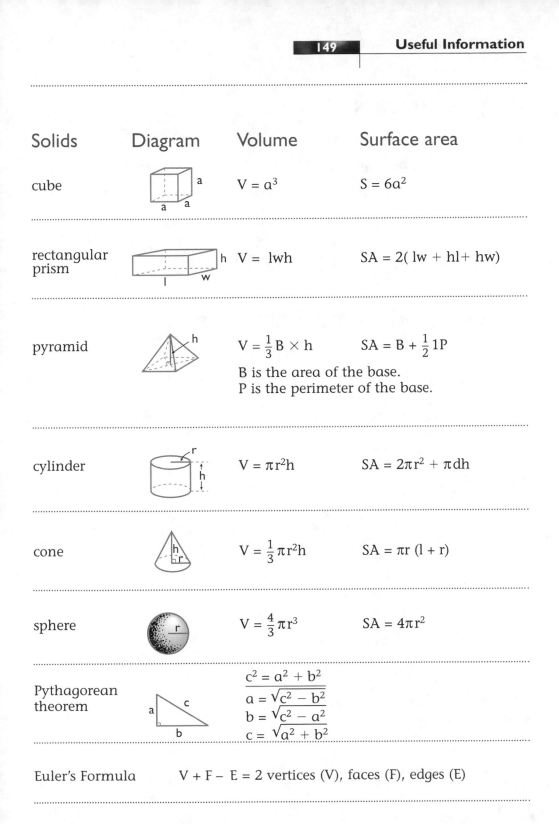

Solids	Diagram	Volume	Surface area
cube		$V = a^3$	$S = 6a^2$
rectangular prism		$V = lwh$	$SA = 2(lw + hl + hw)$
pyramid		$V = \frac{1}{3}B \times h$ B is the area of the base. P is the perimeter of the base.	$SA = B + \frac{1}{2}lP$
cylinder		$V = \pi r^2 h$	$SA = 2\pi r^2 + \pi dh$
cone		$V = \frac{1}{3}\pi r^2 h$	$SA = \pi r (l + r)$
sphere		$V = \frac{4}{3}\pi r^3$	$SA = 4\pi r^2$
Pythagorean theorem		$c^2 = a^2 + b^2$ $a = \sqrt{c^2 - b^2}$ $b = \sqrt{c^2 - a^2}$ $c = \sqrt{a^2 + b^2}$	

Euler's Formula $V + F - E = 2$ vertices (V), faces (F), edges (E)

large numbers

million	$1,000 \times 1,000$	10^6
billion	1,000 millions	10^9
trillion	1,000 billions	10^{12}
quadrillion	million billions	10^{15}

letters used in mathematics

In sets:

I	integers
N	natural numbers
Q	rational numbers
R	real numbers
W	whole numbers

In geometry:

a, b, c, d, ...	sides of polygons
	lengths of intervals
	names of lines
A, B, C, D, ...	points, vertices
A	area of polygons
b	base of polygons
B	area of the base
C	circumference of a circle
d	diameter of a circle
h	height
l	length
P	perimeter
r	radius of a circle
s	side
SA	surface area
V	volume of solids
w	width

decimal system prefixes

Prefix	Symbol	Value	Value in words	Example	Meaning
pico	p	10^{-12}	one trillionth of	1 pF	picofarad
nano	n	10^{-9}	one thousand millionth of	1 ns	nanosecond
micro	μ	10^{-6}	one millionth of	1 μs	microsecond
milli	m	10^{-3}	one thousandth of	1 mg	milligram
centi	c	10^{-2}	one hundredth of	1 cm	centimeter
deci	d	10^{-1}	one tenth of	1 dB	decibel
			one		
deca	d, D	10^{1}	10 times	1 dag	decagram
hecto	h	10^{2}	100 times	1 hL	hectoliter
kilo	k	10^{3}	1,000 times	1 kg	kilogram
mega	M	10^{6}	1 million times	1 ML	megaliter
giga	G	10^{9}	1 thousand million times	1 GB	gigabyte

numerical prefixes

Prefix	Meaning	Example
mono	1	monorail
bi	2	bicycle, binary
tri	3	tricycle, triangle
tetra	4	tetrahedron, tetrapack
quad	4	quadrilateral, quads
penta, quin	5	pentagon
hexa	6	hexagon
hepta, septi	7	heptagon
octa	8	octagon
nona, nov	9	nonagon
deca	10	decagon, decahedron
undeca	11	undecagon
dodeca	12	dodecagon, dodecahedron
icosa	20	icosahedron
hect	100	hectare
kilo	1,000	kilogram
mega	1,000,000	megaliter, megawatt
giga	1,000 million	gigabyte

other prefixes

Prefix	Meaning	Example
anti	opposite, against	counterclockwise
circum	around	circumference
co	together	cointerior, coordinate
geo	earth	geometry
hemi	half	hemisphere
macro	very big	macrocosmos
micro	very small	microbe
multi	many, much	multibase blocks
peri	around	perimeter
poly	many	polygon
semi	half	semicircle
sub	below, under	subset
trans	across, beyond, over	transversal
uni	one, having one	one

the multiplication square

×	1	2	3	4	5	6	7	8	9	10
1	1	2	3	4	5	6	7	8	9	10
2	2	4	6	8	10	12	14	16	18	20
3	3	6	9	12	15	18	21	24	27	30
4	4	8	12	16	20	24	28	32	36	40
5	5	10	15	20	25	30	35	40	45	50
6	6	12	18	24	30	36	42	48	54	60
7	7	14	21	28	35	42	49	56	63	70
8	8	16	24	32	40	48	56	64	72	80
9	9	18	27	36	45	54	63	72	81	90
10	10	20	30	40	50	60	70	80	90	100

Greek alphabet

The letters of the Greek alphabet are used as symbols for angles, mathematical operations, etc.

Examples:

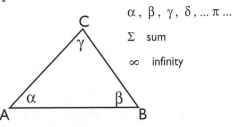

α, β, γ, δ, ... π ...

Σ sum

∞ infinity

Capital	Lower case	Handwritten	Pronunciation
A	α	α	alpha
B	β	β	beta
Γ	γ	γ	gamma
Δ	δ	δ	delta
E	ϵ	ε	epsilon
Z	ζ	ζ	zeta
H	η	η	eta
Θ	θ	θ	theta
I	ι	ι	iota
K	κ	κ	kappa
Λ	λ	λ	lambda
M	μ	μ	mu
N	ν	ν	nu
Ξ	ξ	ξ	xi
O	o	o	omicron
Π	π	π	pi
P	ρ	ρ	rho
Σ	σ	σ	sigma
T	τ	τ	tau
Υ	υ	u	upsilon
Φ	ϕ	φ	phi
X	χ	x	chi
Ψ	ψ	ψ	psi
Ω	ω	ω	omega